THE PSYCHOLOGY OF CHESS

Do you need to be a genius to be good at chess? What does it take to become a grandmaster? Can computer programmes beat human intuition in gameplay?

The Psychology of Chess is an insightful overview of the roles of intelligence, expertise and human intuition in playing this complex and ancient game. The book explores the idea of "practice makes perfect", alongside accounts of why men perform better than women in international rankings, and why chess has become synonymous with extreme intelligence as well as madness.

When artificial intelligence researchers are increasingly studying chess to develop machine learning, *The Psychology of Chess* shows us how much chess has already taught us about the human mind.

Fernand Gobet is Professor of Decision Making and Expertise at the University of Liverpool, UK. He is a chess international master, and played numerous times for the Swiss national team.

THE PSYCHOLOGY OF EVERYTHING

The Psychology of Everything is a series of books which debunk the myths and pseudo-science surrounding some of life's biggest questions.

The series explores the hidden psychological factors that drive us, from our sub-conscious desires and aversions, to the innate social instincts handed to us across the generations. Accessible, informative, and always intriguing, each book is written by an expert in the field, examining how research-based knowledge compares with popular wisdom, and illustrating the potential of psychology to enrich our understanding of humanity and modern life.

Applying a psychological lens to an array of topics and contemporary concerns – from sex to addiction to conspiracy theories – The Psychology of Everything will make you look at everything in a new way.

Titles in the series

The Psychology of Grief
Richard Gross

The Psychology of Sex
Meg-John Barker

The Psychology of Dieting
Jane Ogden

The Psychology of Performance
Stewart T. Cotterill

The Psychology of Trust
Ken J. Rotenberg

The Psychology of Working Life
Toon Taris

The Psychology of Conspiracy Theories
Jan-Willem van Prooijen

The Psychology of Addiction
Jenny Svanberg

The Psychology of Fashion
Carolyn Mair

The Psychology of Gardening
Harriet Gross

The Psychology of Gender
Gary W. Wood

The Psychology of Climate Change
Geoffrey Beattie

For further information about this series please visit:
www.thepsychologyofeverything.co.uk

THE PSYCHOLOGY OF CHESS

FERNAND GOBET

Routledge
Taylor & Francis Group

LONDON AND NEW YORK

First published 2019
by Routledge
2 Park Square, Milton Park, Abingdon, Oxon OX14 4RN

and by Routledge
711 Third Avenue, New York, NY 10017

Routledge is an imprint of the Taylor & Francis Group, an informa business

British Library Cataloguing-in-Publication Data
A catalogue record for this book is available from the British Library

Library of Congress Cataloging-in-Publication Data
Names: Gobet, Fernand, author.
Title: The psychology of chess / Fernand Gobet.
Description: New York : Routledge, 2019. | Series: The Psychology
    of Everything
Identifiers: LCCN 2018020887 (print) | LCCN 2018024430 (ebook) |
    ISBN 9781315441863 (ePub) | ISBN 9781315441870 (Adobe) |
    ISBN 9781315441856 (Mobipocket) | ISBN 9781138216631
    (Hardback) | ISBN 9781138216655 (Paperback) |
    ISBN 9781315441887 (eBook)
Subjects: LCSH: Chess—Psychological aspects.
Classification: LCC GV1448 (ebook) | LCC GV1448 .G634 2019 (print) |
    DDC 794.1019—dc23
LC record available at https://lccn.loc.gov/2018020887

ISBN: 978-1-138-21663-1 (hbk)
ISBN: 978-1-138-21665-5 (pbk)
ISBN: 978-1-315-44188-7 (ebk)

Typeset in Joanna
by Apex CoVantage, LLC

To the Queens of my Life

Chess is like life.
World champion Boris Spassky

Chess is life.
World champion Bobby Fischer

Chess is not life.
World champion Hou Yifan

CONTENTS

PREFACE

This book is a non-technical introduction to the psychology of chess. It is a book I thought of writing many years ago. Thirty years ago, to be precise, when I started working on my PhD on chess players' memory. At the time, I decided that not enough was known about the topic to write such a book, and that I should wait a few more years.

The wait took longer than expected. Although I did write three monographs on chess memory and board games, and two introductions to the psychology of expertise, I never went back to the original idea.

When Ceri McLardy invited me to write a short book on the topic for the series *The Psychology of Everything*, I accepted immediately – I could not wait any longer! Besides, now we do know quite a lot about the psychology of chess.

The book is aimed at three main audiences. First, undergraduate students. For this audience, general implications for psychology will be drawn from chess research. Second, general readers interested in the psychology of chess. Several of the selected themes will be of directed interest to them. Third, chess players who want to understand the psychological mechanisms underpinning the way they think when playing chess. Sections on errors, style, intuition and training will be of particular interest to them. Knowledge of the rules of the game is not necessary to enjoy this book, and care has been taken not to use chess jargon, or to explain it when it is used. No background in psychology is expected, either.

In line with this collection, the number of references is kept to a minimum. The suggested items in the Further Reading section at the end of the book provide sources where detailed pointers to the literature can be found.

Around the time of my PhD, I had the very good fortune of collaborating with Adriaan de Groot and Herbert Simon, two outstanding scientists who made seminal contributions to the psychology of chess. Later, I trained several gifted researchers (Merim Bilalić, Guillermo Campitelli, Philippe Chassy and Giovanni Sala) who had decided to devote their PhD research to aspects of chess psychology. Both the old and new research will be described in this book.

In my first career, I was a professional chess player, reaching the title of an international master and playing for the Swiss national team. Therefore, I have sometimes taken the liberty of providing first-hand evidence and insights about chess players and their mind.

ACKNOWLEDGEMENTS

Many thanks to Guillermo Campitelli, Philippe Chassy, Morgan Ereku, Alexey Root and Giovanni Sala for their comments on a draft of this book and many exciting discussions about chess psychology.

OPENING

Chess fascinates many people, even those who do not play it. It is played at all ages, in all countries, without any attention to religion or ethnic background. As a symbol of intelligence and good decision-making, it is often used in advertisements for banking and business. As a symbol of genius bordering on madness, it is a common theme in fiction and has generated numerous books and movies.

Born in India in the 6th century, chess was adopted in Persia (Iran) in the next century, and then by the Arabs. The first books on chess were written in the 9th century, but did not survive to our day. It is also in the 9th century that chess was introduced to Europe, through Spain and Sicily. By the 13th century, chess was the dominant game in Europe, as witnessed in the *Book of Games*, written in 1283 at the request of Alfonso X of Castile: "Since chess is the noblest game, which requires the most skill compared to all the other games, we are going to talk about it first of all". By then, its influence had spread well beyond the sphere of games and it was part of culture at large. For example, in the second half of the 13th century, Jacobus de Cessolis, an Italian monk, preached morality using chess as metaphor: "In life, as on the chessboard, each piece has its own rights but also its own obligations".

Chess has sometimes been the mirror of historical developments. At the end of the 15th century, at a time when women were gaining importance in politics in medieval Europe, the rules of the game changed, and the until-then modest vizier – who could move only one square diagonally – mutated into the powerful queen, who can move in any direction without any limitation. Anticipating the French Revolution by 40 years, François-André Danican Philidor, the best player of the time and an opera composer, asserted that the pawns (the weakest of the chess pieces) were not just cannon fodder, but actually were the "soul of chess". This paved the way for the scientific approach to chess, and in particular the theory developed by Wilhelm Steinitz. The impact of his approach on chess has been compared to the impact of Newtonian theory in physics.

At the height of the Cold War, the match between American Bobby Fischer and Soviet Boris Spassky captured the imagination of the public. So did the matches between political refugee Viktor Korchnoi and Soviet apparatchik Anatoly Karpov, spiced up by various scandals including the presence of a parapsychologist on Karpov's team allegedly hypnotising his opponent.

In 1997, world champion Garry Kasparov defended the honour of the human race against artificial intelligence in his match against Deep Blue – and lost. This defeat, a milestone in the history of science and technology, led to considerable soul searching in the media and was the inspiration behind several books and movies.

CHESS AND SCIENCE

The nature of chess has been often debated in the literature. It is frequently presented not only as a game, but also as a sport (because of its competitive element), an art (because of the beautiful combinations it allows) and a science (because of the systematic way it is studied).

Although chess players speak of chess "theory", the term is not used in the same way as in science. Rather than a formal system of laws, mechanisms and principles, "theory" in chess means a catalogue of initial moves and their evaluation for the theory of openings, and a discussion of key positions and the way to handle them for the theory of endgames. There were some attempts to identify the fundamental principles of play, most notably by Wilhelm Steinitz, the founder of the classical school of chess, with his 1889 textbook *The Modern Chess Instructor*, and Aron Nimzowitsch, one of the founders of the hypermodern school, with his 1925 book *My System*. However, despite their great originality, both fell short of the rigour of a scientific theory. In addition, what is lacking generally with chess is any effort to test its "theories" in a systematic way, beyond recording new games. Such tests are obviously at the heart of scientific research.

Chess has been the topic of much scientific research. It has been investigated by a number of academic disciplines, including sociology, ethnology, philosophy, mathematics and neuroscience. By far, it is in computer science (including artificial intelligence) and psychology that chess has been studied to the greatest effect. In artificial intelligence, chess has been a standard task for the development of machine learning and search algorithms. In psychology, it has been the topic of seminal research into perception, memory, learning, thinking and decision-making. It has sometimes been called the *drosophila* of cognitive psychology, by analogy to the role of the fruit fly in genetics.

A RICH DOMAIN OF RESEARCH FOR PSYCHOLOGY

Starting with French psychologist Alfred Binet (the creator of the first successful test of intelligence), chess has excited the imagination of psychologists. Binet studied blindfold chess, a variant of chess where players do not see the board. In 1925, a group of Russian psychologists took advantage of the Moscow tournament, which brought together the best players of the time, to administer a battery of psychometric tests, measuring abilities such as memory, intelligence and even motivation with the Rorschach test. They found that there was hardly any difference between chess masters and a control group matched for intelligence, except for tests using chess material and tests measuring the ability to distribute attention and discover logical principles. They also provided a list of the physical and mental qualities required by chess, which were instrumental in convincing the Soviet government that chess should be encouraged as an activity leading to the development of self-discipline and the improvement of intellectual competences.

However, it is to Dutch psychologist and chess master Adriaan de Groot that we owe the first experimental study on chess psychology, which he carried out for his PhD research. In 1938, he was earning money as a journalist by covering the AVRO tournament in Amsterdam, which brought together the world's best eight players. He managed to convince five of the participants to take part in his experiments, including world champions Alexander Alekhine and Max Euwe. Amusingly, some of the data were collected after the tournament on the steamer carrying many European masters to Buenos Aires, where the 1939 Olympiads (world championship by teams) were held. As the trip was rather long, players were grateful to participate in these experiments and therefore to break the monotony of the voyage.

De Groot studied not only chess players' ability to find good moves, but also their ability to rapidly understand the gist of a position even after seeing it just for a few seconds, as well as their ability to memorise these positions rapidly and accurately. Many of the ideas presented in this book can be traced backed to de Groot's PhD thesis.

The second key study in chess psychology, carried out by Herbert Simon and William Chase in 1973 at Carnegie Mellon University in Pittsburgh, developed a powerful theory – called chunking theory – to explain de Groot's data. Combining experimental methods with ideas from artificial intelligence and computational modelling, Simon and Chase performed a series of experiments that inspired much of the research carried out in the following decades.

Nowadays, chess psychology is an active domain of research and is arguably still the main domain in expertise research. Many different aspects of chess are studied, from cognition to personality to intelligence. Several reasons explain this popularity, including: chess has its own rating system, the Elo rating, which offers a precise and up-to-date measure of skill; it has an ideal balance between simplicity and complexity; it allows many experimental manipulations; and it has strong external validity. In fact, the key discoveries made in chess psychology generalise to most domains of expertise, and indeed to psychology in general, as we shall see. Thus, researchers often study chess not for its own sake, but for understanding expertise in general.

PREVIEW OF BOOK

The following three chapters cover standard topics in cognitive psychology: perception, learning, memory and decision-making. They are anchored in the work of de Groot, Simon and Chase. Chapter 4 discusses the relative roles of practice and talent, and emphasises the importance of studying their interaction. Chapter 5 tries to understand why men appear to perform better than women in chess at the top level. The following three chapters are devoted to applied chess psychology, and cover topics such as errors, style, intuition, training, psychological warfare and cheating. The discussion of style and intuition will draw on recent developments in artificial intelligence, focusing on what they tell us about human psychology. Chapter 9 examines the possible benefits of playing chess (e.g. for education or psychotherapy) and Chapter 10 addresses the potential costs (e.g. the hypothesis that there is a link between madness and chess).

APPENDIX: A VERY SHORT INTRODUCTION TO CHESS

In this book, chess refers to international chess, which is distinct from Japanese chess (shogi) and Chinese chess (shiang qi). Chess is a game played on an 8 × 8 board. The aim of the game is to capture (checkmate) the opponent's king. At the beginning of the game, each player, called White and Black, has eight pieces and eight pawns. The White pieces are placed on the first row in the following order: rook, knight, bishop, queen, king, bishop, knight and rook. The White pawns are placed on the second row. The Black pieces and pawns are placed in the same way on the eighth and seventh row. Rooks move horizontally and vertically, and bishops move diagonally. The queen, the most powerful piece, moves horizontally, vertically and diagonally. The king moves one square in any direction. The knight moves two squares horizontally (or vertically), and then one square vertically (or horizontally), thus forming an L shape. Unlike the other pieces, it can jump over other pieces. If a move ends on a square occupied by an opponent's piece, this piece is removed from the board (captured). Pawns move one square forward (from their starting square, they can also move two squares forward) and capture one square diagonally. Additional rules include castling (a move where both the king and a rook move simultaneously), taking *en passant* (a pawn moving two squares from its starting position can be captured by an opponent's pawn as if it had moved only one square), stalemate (if one side cannot move but is not in check, then the game is a draw) and pawn promotion (when a pawn reaches the end of the board, it may be replaced by a stronger piece of the same colour).

White moves first, which provides a small advantage. A typical game can be divided into three phases, although the boundaries are often fuzzy: the opening (the first moves of the game where each side develops their pieces), the middle game (where each side manoeuvres to gain a material or positional advantage whilst thwarting the opponent's objectives) and the endgame (where few pieces and pawns remain on the board).

To record games, chess players use the algebraic notation, where the letters refer to files and numbers to rows. Pieces (except pawns) are indicated by their initial letter, with N being used for "knight" to avoid confusion with "king". For example, the first moves of the shortest possible game are written as 1.f3 e5 2.g4 Qh4 checkmate.

Chess skill is measured with the Elo rating, a method invented by Arpad Elo. It is an interval scale with a theoretical mean of 1500 and a theoretical standard deviation of 200. The following skill levels are often used (with the Elo range in parentheses): class D players (1200–1400), class C players (1400–1600), class B players (1600–1800), class A players (1800–2000), experts or candidate masters (2000–2200), masters (2200–2400), international masters (2400–2500) and grandmasters (above 2500).

1

THE EYE OF THE MASTER

Anybody who has seen chess masters playing bullet chess (1 minute per side for the entire game) or simultaneous exhibitions, where they play against 30 or 40 opponents at the same time, would have been struck by their amazing ability to play good moves very quickly. Indeed, the quality of moves played under these taxing conditions is surprisingly high, although not as high as with games played under normal conditions (on average, 3 minutes per move). It is as if masters *see* the board differently than weaker players. Where novices see wooden or plastic pieces, masters see trajectories, ideas, concepts and sequences of moves. In fact, the same applies in other fields: one of the hallmarks of experts in science, medicine and sport is the ability to rapidly perceive the key features of a problem.

The first person to have addressed this question empirically was Adriaan de Groot in his doctoral dissertation, originally published in Dutch in 1946 and translated in English in 1965. Because of the number of issues it addressed and its strong scientific impact, this work has become a classic in psychology.

A BETTER UNDERSTANDING AFTER 5 SECONDS THAN AFTER 15 MINUTES!

De Groot's main interest concerned the processes that allow chess players to choose a move. Specifically, he wanted to test the hypothesis that, compared to amateurs, chess masters considered more positions when they were looking ahead and that they anticipated longer sequences of moves – that is, they were searching deeper. In a first experiment, he gave chess players a board position unknown to them and asked them to select what they thought was the best move. He also asked them to say aloud what they were thinking about. The players consisted of amateurs, candidate masters and world-class grandmasters, including world champions. The transcripts of players' utterances – called verbal protocols – were then analysed in great detail, both qualitatively and quantitatively.

The results did not support his expectations: although grandmasters played better moves, they did not differ substantially from other players with respect to structural variables such as the depth of search, the number of moves considered or the strategies used when carrying out search (see Chapter 3 for details). There was an important difference, however. The best players were able to pinpoint promising solutions very rapidly, which allowed them to narrow down their search drastically. As de Groot put it, the world champion understood the problem position better *after 5 seconds* than a candidate master *after 15 minutes!* This was fully unexpected. What was critical was not the detail of the way players analysed the position by trying out different moves, sometimes for more than 30 minutes. Rather, the difference resided in the very first few seconds of seeing a position: perception is central in chess expertise.

In a second experiment, de Groot directly tested this hypothesis. He presented a position briefly, from 2 to 15 seconds, took it away from participants' view, and asked them to reconstruct it as precisely as they could. As expected, grandmasters did much better than candidate masters, who in turn did better than amateurs. Whilst a grandmaster could reconstruct nearly the entire position correctly, a strong amateur struggled to remember half of the pieces.

De Groot explored several variants of this experiment. In some versions, he asked players to think aloud, either during the presentation of the position, immediately after or 30 seconds after. From the protocols, it is clear that experts did not see individual pieces, but rather saw large complexes, in which perceptual aspects are inter-twined with dynamic possibilities. In fact, they rarely perceived static groups of pieces, but almost always threats, probable moves and even sequences of moves. Note that this is the case even when players are told explicitly beforehand that the task is to recall a position, and not to find the best move.

I will have more to say about this experiment in Chapter 2, but for the time being it is important to realise that this task was in de Groot's mind a *perceptual* task, the aim of which was to understand what grandmasters *saw* during the first seconds they looked at an unknown position. Later on, this task became highly popular and in more recent research has been predominantly used for studying memory.

RECORDING EYE MOVEMENTS

A natural way to study skill differences in perception is to record eye movements. This technology was not available before the war when de Groot collected the data of his PhD research, and it is only in the 1960s that he was able to carry out such an experiment, with his PhD student Riekent Jongman. The task was again to reproduce a chess position presented briefly, this time uniformly for 5 seconds. The data were fully analysed even later, in a book de Groot wrote with Jong-man and myself (see Further Reading). There were clear differences between weak players and masters, with the latter having shorter and less variable fixations. Masters' fixations also covered more squares and landed more often on the squares that were important from a chess point of view. Another interesting result was that masters fixated more often on the intersection of squares than the weak players. This buttresses the hypothesis that masters perceive groups of pieces rather than individual pieces. Finally, it is likely that fairly simple visual cues – such as a White pawn that has penetrated Black's defence – direct masters' eye movements to significant squares. In chess, per-ceptually salient features correlate very often with the strategic and tactical meanings of a position.

Just like some of the old experiments, the eye-movement experiments used verbal protocols. After reconstructing a position – more or less successfully – players were requested to retrospect on what they had seen during its presentation. In general, masters' retrospective descriptions broadly agreed with the actual sequence of eye fixations. An interesting exception was that, in the cases where they had fixated the same square several times, players tended to remember only the first fixation. The same finding has been documented in experiments measuring memory for sequences of words, where repeated items tend to be recalled poorly – a phenomenon known as the Ranschburg effect. The protocols were also useful for providing information about where players directed their attention and about the way they dealt with atypical positions (e.g. positions that cannot be put in standard categories).

Later experiments measuring eye movements have also produced striking skill differences. For example, Charness and colleagues used a problem-solving task in which participants (intermediate players and candidate masters) had to find the winning move in a position. In addition to being faster and choosing better moves, the candidate masters had fewer fixations but larger eye movements than the intermediate players. Their first fixations tended to land on empty squares more often, and, when considering fixations on pieces only, they fixated on important pieces more frequently. In general, the data supported the idea that strong players combined perceptual knowledge with the information provided by peripheral vision to direct their eye movements.

PERCEPTION: INCREMENTAL AND ANTICIPATORY

A classic debate in psychology concerns the nature of perception: is it holistic, with objects perceived in their totality, as maintained by Gestalt psychologists, or is it constructed by incremental mechanisms, as argued by reductionists? Although not a Gestalt psychologist himself, de Groot proposed that strong players start with a "landscape view" of the board, which provides a global impression of the position, with the details omitted. In the 1960s, there was an interesting debate about this issue between Soviet psychologist Oleg Tikhomirov and Herbert Simon, with Tikhomirov defending the view that perception is holistic, while Simon argued that local mechanisms (e.g. perception of relations of defence and attack between pieces) were sufficient for explaining the data. More recently, Gobet and Chassy run computer simulations based on the idea of chunks and templates (see the next chapter), showing that experts' perception, even though it might look holistic, can be accounted for by the incremental construction of an internal representation using patterns that are initially fairly small.

Another idea proposed by de Groot seems better supported by the empirical evidence. He suggested that chess masters used *anticipatory schemas*. These dynamic schemas contain information allowing players to anticipate potential actions. As experts have more and better developed schemas, they can anticipate actions better. Vincent Ferrari and colleagues at the University of Provence (France) tested this hypothesis. In a first experiment, players saw two positions in quick succession and had to say whether the second position was the same as the first one. The results showed that strong amateurs performed better when the two positions appeared as a normal sequence of moves, unlike beginners who could not use information about the normality of moves.

In a second experiment, Ferrari and colleagues studied whether players tend to recall positions as they were shown or, rather, the positions that would occur after the standard move is played, as predicted by the presence of anticipatory schemas. A recognition task was used. Players saw 10 chess positions displayed in succession; half of the positions were standard opening situations, while the other half were a different set of opening situations, this time with one additional move played. During the recognition phase, players were presented with 10 old positions (the positions they had seen in the first phase of the experiment) and 10 new positions (half were the positions they had seen plus one standard move, and the other half were the positions they had seen minus the standard move). The results showed that the strongest players (class A players) made many false recognitions, where they recalled not the position they had seen, but the position after the normal move had been made. The beauty of this experiment is that better players committed more false recognitions than weaker players, showing that in some circumstances expert perception can lead to errors. In sum, these two experiments back up the hypothesis that experts use anticipatory schemas in their perception: rather than recalling a scene the way they saw it, experts tend to recall it the way it normally unfolds in the near future.

PERCEPTION IS COGNITION

The importance and speed of perception is not limited to chess, but has been documented in many other domains of expertise, such as music, medicine, sports and driving. In all these domains, experts literally *see* a different problem situation and categorise it in a better way. Rather than being innate, experts' perception is the product of many years of practice and study. One of de Groot's major contributions is to have shown that there is no clear boundary between perception and cognition: in chess and in other domains, perception, memory and problem-solving are tightly interconnected.

2

CHUNKS!

De Groot uncovered some fascinating phenomena, but his work was essentially descriptive and his theoretical explanations were not compelling. The first theory to convincingly account for de Groot's results was proposed by Herbert Simon and William Chase in 1973 in three classic papers, in what is known as the *chunking theory*. The theory was primarily aimed at explaining two phenomena: chess experts' remarkable memory and their ability to find good moves rapidly — as de Groot put it, strong chess players automatically see the good move. Chunking theory's strength is to have proposed fairly detailed mechanisms to explain these phenomena. The fact that Simon was one of the founders of artificial intelligence and modern cognitive psychology was not an incidental factor to the strength of chunking theory. Indeed, Simon had previously built several computational models that captured some of the ideas he developed with Chase. Chunking theory, as well as the empirical work that supported it, motivated a considerable amount of research on expertise in the following twenty years or so.

Chunking theory assumes that chess players encode most of their long-term memory knowledge as chunks — perceptual units that can be treated as wholes. The first chunks are small, but then larger chunks are incrementally built using these smaller chunks. In chess, chunks consist, at the beginning, of individual pieces on a given square, and then grow into groups of pieces. An analogy with reading will make the process clear. At the beginning, a reader learns to recognise individual letters, such as "t" and "h". With practice, these letters form chunks, such as "th", and later "the". The power of chunking is that very large units indeed can be created by this mechanism. So, for example, assuming much practice with reading, the following chunk may be learnt: "To be or not to be, that is the question". Such a chunk is then a unit of both perception and meaning, and can be processed as a whole. Figure 2.1 provides an example of the kinds of chunks learnt by a weak chess player and a master.

In addition to mechanisms explaining how a network of chunks is constructed, the theory made several assumptions about learning and memory. It takes a fairly long time to learn a new chunk (8 seconds) and to add information to a chunk already in long-term memory (2 seconds). But once learnt, chunks can be retrieved rapidly, in a few hundred milliseconds. Short-term memory capacity, which is limited to seven items, is the same for experts and non-experts. Thus, the main difference between weak and strong chess players is the number and size of the chunks they have acquired. A final assumption is that chunks can be linked to information. In chess, this information can

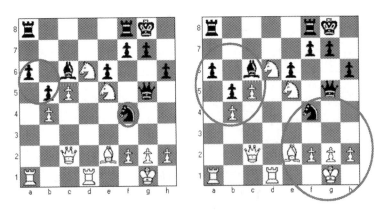

Figure 2.1 Chunks learnt by a weak player (left diagram) and a master (right diagram).

be a move or a sequence of moves, strategic ideas or tactical motifs. For example, given a chunk encoding a pawn structure with a weak square, the suggested action could be: "Place a knight on this square!" In psychology and artificial intelligence such condition-action pairs are known are *productions*.

Chunking theory explains the skill effect in recalling chess positions by assuming that strong players are more likely to recognise chunks on a board position, since they have stored many more chunks in long-term memory. Once a chunk is recognised, a pointer to it is placed in short-term memory. Although only seven pointers can be placed in short-memory, due to its limited capacity, pointers can be associated to small, medium or large chunks. Since strong players have acquired larger chunks than weaker players, they can encode a position with a smaller number of units than weaker players, and can memorise an entire position despite the limited capacity of short-term memory. In sum, while novices perceive a position as a collection of individual pieces, stronger chess players perceive it as collection of familiar configurations.

In work with Kevin Gilmartin, Simon used computer simulations and mathematical extrapolations to estimate that a chess master must have learnt about 50,000 chunks. Simon and Chase note that this number is roughly the same as the number of words that American college students have in their vocabulary. Given the time needed to learn these chunks, they estimated that it takes a minimum of 10 years, or 10,000 hours, to become a chess master.

Simon and Chase also addressed the question of how players use mental imagery to visualise board positions and anticipate moves in their mind's eye. The central idea, already mentioned above, is that potential moves are proposed by pattern recognition: patterns on the board elicit chunks in long-term memory, which in turn suggest possible actions. Chunks also provide information allowing players to reconstruct groups of pieces in their mind's eye. An important aspect of the theory is that pattern recognition occurs not only when looking at a physical board, but also when looking at a board position imagined in the mind's eye. In both cases, recognised chunks might elicit information about what to do in a given situation, including what kind of moves are likely to be good. Thus, this look-ahead search consists of recognising chunks, using the information they provide to update the position in the mind's eye and repeating this process several times. Because chunks provide useful information about moves, plans, tactical motifs, etc., they enable a highly selective search. In sum, chunking theory explains the speed at which expert players find good moves by assuming that chunks allow them (a) to identify patterns on the board; (b) to use these patterns to access useful information, including potentially good moves; and (c) to repeatedly update, after a move has been carried out, the board constructed in their mind's eye and explore the consequences of moves and sequences of moves.

Simon and Chase's theory was very ambitious, since it accounted for data not only about memory, but also about problem-solving. Moreover, it is not limited to chess expertise, but can also be applied to other domains of expertise, and indeed to the study of cognition in general. This explains why it had considerable impact, not only on expertise research, but also on cognitive psychology more generally.

RECALL EXPERIMENT

Simon and Chase's genius was not only to have proposed a powerful theory, but also to have supported it empirically with elegant experiments. They focused on de Groot's perception task – which they considered as a *recall task* – providing both a replication and an extension. A chessboard was shown for five seconds, after which players attempted to reconstruct it. There were two important differences in comparison to de Groot's experiment. First, Simon and Chase did not ask participants to think aloud during the experiment. Second, in addition to board positions taken from masters' games, they used random positions, where the pieces of a game position were haphazardly placed on the board. The results showed that there was a skill effect with positions taken from games, but not random positions.

An interesting feature of Simon and Chase's study is that there were only three participants. The master was Hans Berliner, a former world chess champion by correspondence – a variant of chess where moves are transmitted through post – who was a PhD student in computer science at Carnegie Mellon University. The class A player was William Chase himself. While Chase was aware of the hypotheses being tested, the positions were not selected by him, for obvious reasons. The beginner was Micheline Chi, a PhD student in psychology, who later married Chase. The small sample was compensated by very detailed analyses, which tested very specific theoretical questions. This study is a nice example of the fact that experiments with very small sample sizes can lead to powerful results, which in this case started a very influential tradition of research.

COPY TASK

In comparison to the original study, another important addition was a *copy task*, which provided critical information about the structure of chunks. In this task, players could still see the stimulus board when the position was reconstructed on a second board. So, typically, players would glance at the stimulus board, direct their attention to the reconstruction board and place a few pieces, glance again at the stimulus board, and place yet more pieces. Simon and Chase used the fact that the two boards could not be fixated at the same time to provide an empirical operationalisation of a chunk: pieces replaced together after a glance at the stimulus board belong to the same chunk. Thus, complementing the first definition of a chunk as a group of pieces, we now have here a second definition.

Simon and Chase also studied the latencies between the placements of two pieces. They reasoned that, if two pieces belong to the same chunk, they should be replaced rapidly together. By contrast, if two pieces belong to two different chunks, the latency between them should be longer. As predicted, most of the pieces within a chunk – as defined by whether players glanced or not at the stimulus board – were replaced in less than 2 seconds, while the pieces that belonged to two different chunks were replaced in more than 2 seconds. In addition, the distributions of placement times between the recall and the copy task were essentially the same. Thus, one can assume that the same process occurs in the recall and the copy task. Here, we have a third definition of a chunk: the 2-second threshold between the placement of two pieces.

Finally, Simon and Chase used chess semantics to define a chunk. They counted the number of chess relations shared by two pieces placed in succession. There were five relations: colour, defence, attack, proximity and kind. Simon and Chase found that two pieces placed in succession shared more chess relations with each other when they were part of a chunk than when they belonged to two different chunks. The beauty of Simon and Chase's research is that the three empirical definitions of a chunk – glances at the stimulus board, latencies and number of relations – provided very consistent results.

DIRECT SUPPORT FOR CHUNKING HYPOTHESIS

As discussed below, Simon and Chase's study has been replicated with larger samples and a tighter methodology. In addition, the expertise effect in recalling chess material is robust and has been obtained even when the experimental method is changed in various ways. For example, the effect remains when the presentation times are varied from 1 second to 60 seconds, when positions come from openings, middlegames and endgames or when positions are presented on diagrams where chess pieces are replaced by letters. The skill effect has also been found in nearly all domains of expertise, including games, sports, science and the arts.

The chunking hypothesis has also been directly confirmed in several experiments. The earliest support, and one of the most convincing, was provided by Neil Charness in his PhD thesis. He dictated positions using the notation used by chess players, at the pace of just above 2 seconds per piece. The pieces were grouped during dictation, using three different orders. In the first condition, Charness used the kind of chunks defined by Simon and Chase; in the second condition, the pieces were dictated file by file; in the final condition, the pieces were presented randomly. In line with chunking theory, players recalled the positions best when the pieces were dictated using chunks. Random order yielded the worst recall. In another experiment, Charness presented the pieces visually, with the same results. These experiments are important, because the variable of interest – whether pieces belonged to the same chunk or not – was controlled by the experimenter.

PROBLEMS WITH THE THEORY

Unfortunately, several experimental findings turned out to be inconsistent with chunking theory. In fact, there were two anomalies in Simon and Chase's own results. The first was that the largest chunks replaced by their master were not that large: a maximum of 5–6 pieces. The second anomaly was that the master and class A player employed more chunks than the novice. In all cases, the number of chunks did not exceed the postulated capacity of short-term memory (7 ± 2), but this result could be an indication that stronger players' short-term memory has a larger capacity, contrary to the prediction of the theory.

Although they raised a lot of theoretical debate and led to numerous experiments, these two anomalies were in reality an artefact of the way Simon and Chase presented the positions, using a standard chessboard and pieces. The issue here is that the hand can only hold a limited number of pieces; thus, even if players recognise large chunks, these are going to be split in smaller chunks. This explanation was confirmed by two experiments I carried out, the first with Herbert Simon himself, and the second with Gary Clarkson, who was an undergraduate student at the University of Nottingham. In the first experiment, a computer display was used to present the positions and record the participants' reconstructions. We also had a much larger sample than in the original study. This time, masters replaced very large chunks, containing up to 19 pieces – about three times larger than what Simon and Chase had found. Also, the number of chunks replaced did not differ between players of different skill levels.

In the second experiment, we found direct support for the hypothesis that the capacity of the hand confounded Simon and Chase's results. Players performed the copy and the recall task, both with a physical board and a computer display. Just like with Simon and Chase's study, the physical display led to relatively small chunks. And just like with the replication I did with Simon, the computer display led to fairly large chunks. It should be noted that the presence of large chunks is consistent with the way chess masters describe their games, as was documented in the verbal protocols collected by de Groot. Masters employ high-level concepts, in some cases characterising the entire board. For example: "a queen's gambit defence, with White carrying out a minority attack and Black having a passive position".

While the anomalies in Simon and Chase's data were artefacts, other findings posed genuine challenges for chunking theory. A first recalcitrant result was uncovered by Neil Charness, again in his PhD research. As we saw earlier, two of the assumptions of chunking theory are that short-term memory has limited capacity and chunks are encoded in long-term memory relatively slowly. When these two assumptions are combined, a strong prediction is that short-term memory should be highly sensitive to interferences. Thus, interpolating a task between the presentation of a chessboard and its reconstruction should lead to a drastic loss of performance. This is because the pointers to long-term memory are erased by the second task; since learning new information is slow, there is not enough time to encode the board in long-term memory. In fact, this is what happens with the recall of words when interpolated tasks are used. However, contrary to the prediction of chunking theory, Charness found that the interfering task decreased performance only by about 10%, which is relatively small. Even using chess tasks as interference, such as finding the winning move in a second position, did not affect the recall of the first position much.

One way of creating interference is to ask players to recall two, three or more positions. The positions that come later in the sequence can be considered as interfering tasks for the positions that came earlier (retro-active interference). Indeed, retaining the earlier positions also interferes with the memory of the positions that come after (proactive interference). Again, chunking theory predicts that recall of all positions should become increasingly poorer as the number of boards increases. Several authors carried out the experiment, and the results showed that, while the task was too hard for amateurs, masters can do it relatively well, even though there seems to be a barrier after five boards.

A REVISION OF CHUNKING THEORY

Chunking theory did a good job at explaining some of the empirical data, but failed to account for the lack of interference effects. Could it be modified so that its weaknesses are corrected whilst its strengths are maintained? This was the aim of template theory, which I developed with Simon. The key idea was to offer mechanisms explaining how high-level memory structures (schemas) are unconsciously created from simpler memory structures (chunks). There is substantial empirical evidence that people use schemas: these are structures where some parts are invariable, while some parts are variable. A good example is the schema of a house. A house normally has a floor, a ceiling and a roof; this is the fixed part of the schema. In addition, some components might or might not be present (such as a garage, an en-suite and a basement), and the number of some components might vary (such as the number of doors and windows); this is the variable part of the schema.

Template theory keeps the idea of chunks but also proposes that templates — which are a kind of schema — are created when some chunks are used frequently. The core of the template, which is a chunk, consists of stable information. The slots consist of information that is variable. For example, in chess, a slot could be created for some pieces that are important, given the presence of the chunk in the core, but that can be located on different squares. Similarly, a slot could be created for an important square that could be occupied by different pieces. The theory assumes that information can be encoded rapidly in the slots, in about 250 milliseconds. Thus, the presence of templates accounts for the results of the interference and multiple-board experiments not only by providing fairly large memory structures, but also by assuming rapid encoding into long-term memory, thus side-stepping the limited capacity of short-term memory. Importantly, templates can be used to store domain specific information only. Thus, chess experts can use them to memorise chess positions, but not lists of words. Just like chunks, templates also provide useful information for decision-making, such as plausible moves and standard plans. In particular, they allow search to be carried out in a more abstract space than considering concrete moves. As documented in verbal protocols, strong players often carry out search using key points of a game. For example, a standard plan for Black in the Benoni defence is (a) to expand on the queen's side, (b) to exchange pieces and (c) to win the endgame due to the pawn majority on the queen's side. The claim is that templates offer the type of information necessary for carrying out this kind of abstract search.

Thus, template theory postulates more learning mechanisms than chunking theory. In addition to chunks and productions, already present in the original theory, template theory postulates that templates must be acquired, and so must links connecting chunks and templates together if they are similar enough. Constructing such a network, which is more complex than that proposed by chunking theory, explains why it takes several years of study and practice to become an expert in chess and other complex domains.

The great strength of template theory is that it is implemented as a computer programme (CHREST: Chunk Hierarchies and REtrieval STructures), which guarantees that all the postulated mechanisms are specified in detail (if they are left unspecified, then the programme will not run). All the learning mechanisms mentioned in the previous section are implemented, as well as mechanisms for managing short-term memory and focusing attention through eye movements. Importantly, all the learning is done automatically, simulating the unconscious acquisition and use of knowledge by human players.

CHREST has simulated several of the empirical data I have reviewed in this and the preceding chapter. From beginners to grandmasters, it replicates the percentage of pieces correctly recalled, the way pieces are chunked during reconstruction and the type of errors made. It also simulates how different types of positions (e.g. positions taken from masters' games, positions modified by mirror-image and various types of randomised positions) affect recall. It also accounts for how manipulating presentation times from 1 second to 60 seconds affects recall, thus providing support for the validity of CHREST's time parameters, such as the time to create a new chunk (8 seconds), and the time to add information to a template slot (250 milliseconds).

In the previous chapter, I described the clear differences between novices and masters' eye movements when they look for 5 seconds at a new position with the aim of memorising it. CHREST can replicate these differences very well. Just like human players, the simulated masters have shorter fixation times, show less variability in the duration of their fixations, tend to fixate important squares and fixate more squares as well as more important squares. These results are partly due to the fact that, while the novice version relies exclusively on simple but relatively slow rules of thumb (e.g. fixate the centre) to direct eye movements, the master version can also use the information contained in chunks, which enables faster fixations as they are automatic. As more chunks have been learnt, more fixations are directed by the structure of chunks in long-term memory.

CHREST has also accounted for many empirical results beyond chess, such as aspects of expertise in the African game of awele and the East Asian game of Go. Beyond board games, it has simulated phenomena related to concept formation, implicit learning and even acquisition of first language, which can be considered as a kind of expertise.

RECALL OF RANDOM POSITIONS – AN UNEXPECTED BUT CORRECT PREDICTION

An interesting contribution of CHREST is to have made new and counterintuitive predictions that were later supported by the data. Remember that random positions are created by taking the pieces of

 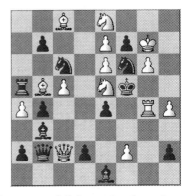

Figure 2.2 Examples of a position taken from a game (left diagram) and a random position (right diagram).

a game position, and randomly placing them on the board (see Figure 2.2 as an example). Remember also that, with random positions, Simon and Chase did not find any difference in performance between their master, class A player and novice. This pattern of results – vast skill differences with game positions, but no differences with random positions – was both spectacular and intuitively satisfying: experts can use their knowledge with structured material but not with unstructured material. It thus found its place in numerous textbooks and popular-science books. The problem is that the second part of the argument (no skill effect with random positions) is not true.

When I was developing CHREST in collaboration with Simon, the programme consistently and stubbornly predicted that masters should remember random positions better than weaker players, even though the absolute number of pieces remembered should be much smaller than with game positions. In one of the rare cases where his scientific intuition let him down, Simon did not believe the simulations. He thought there were mistakes in the computer programme. There were small mistakes, for sure, but once corrected, the behaviour of the programme was the same: it predicted a skill effect with random positions. The mechanism behind this behaviour was actually simple and a direct consequence of chunking theory. By chance, there are patterns even in random positions, albeit not many of them.

Masters, who have acquired more chunks than weaker players, are more likely to recognise one of these patterns by chance and thus access a chunk in long-term memory. Thus, they should show a small superiority over weaker players.

We combed the literature to find all studies that had used random positions in experiments on chess memory. These positions were typically used as a control task to ascertain that better players do not have a better memory in general. When put together, the results indicated that there is a skill effect even with random positions, even though it was smaller than with game positions. On average, masters recalled about 20 pieces with game positions and five pieces with random positions, while weak amateur (below class B players) recalled five pieces and 2.5 pieces, respectively. In fact, a skill effect was found in 12 out of 13 studies, the exception being Simon and Chase's study! The skill effect did not reach statistical significance in most studies, due to their small sample sizes. In the end, Simon conceded that he should have believed the computer simulations rather than his own intuition.

This result is important theoretically. Not only is it a direct prediction of chunking theory, but it is actually difficult to explain for most theories of expertise – for example, theories that assume that experts' knowledge is primarily coded by relatively high-level memory structures such as schemas. The reason is that small memory structures such as chunks seem necessary for explaining this result.

There is very recent twist in the story. In a meta-analysis of the studies having used random material not only with chess, but with other domains of expertise as well, my PhD student Giovanni Sala found that this skill effect generalises to most domains of expertise, thus providing additional support for the existence of chunking mechanisms in human cognition.

OTHER TYPES OF KNOWLEDGE

Chunks (perceptual knowledge) and potential moves (procedural knowledge) are important kinds of knowledge in chess, but this is not the full picture. Strong chess players possess additional types of knowledge. For example, they have a large stock of declarative knowledge. This includes knowledge of openings (it has been estimated that masters have memorised at least 100,000 opening moves), tactical motifs ("if a piece fulfils several functions and is overloaded, try to take advantage of this"), strategic principles ("two bishops are usually better than two knights") and endgame principles ("passed pawns should usually be advanced"). This also includes an arsenal of techniques and methods such as "if you're one pawn up, try to exchange pieces but not pawns". Note that this declarative knowledge becomes increasingly refined as expertise grows. For example, amateurs usually know that "occupying an open file with rooks is advantageous". Better players, perhaps at master level, have learnt the maxim that "occupying an open file with rooks is advantageous, unless the opponent controls all entry points with minor pieces". Yet a stronger player would know that "occupying an open file with rooks is advantageous, if, in the case where the opponent controls all entry points with minor pieces, it is possible to penetrate the opponent's position with an exchange sacrifice". Some of this knowledge is clearly declarative, but some of it is implicit and encoded in thousands of pairs of chunks/actions. Whatever the type of knowledge, there is the question as to when it is useful and should be acted upon, and when it should better be left alone. It is not uncommon that a small change in the position leads to tactical opportunities that invalidate even the best strategic principles. The answer is that look-ahead search should be carried out to detect such instances.

BLINDFOLD CHESS

There is a variant of chess that supremely taxes memory: blindfold chess. With blindfold chess, one plays without seeing the board, unlike the opponent who, typically, can see it. Players normally communicate using the algebraic notation (e.g. 1. d4 Nf6 2. c4 g6, etc.), which is the standard way of recording moves. As if playing one blindfold game was not difficult enough, it is also possible to play several blindfold games at the same time. Whilst most players above candidate master level can play one blindfold game without too much difficulty, playing several games is a special skill that demands dedicated training. A major difficulty is to keep boards as distinct as possible, which requires a smart choice of openings, for example alternating quiet variations with wild gambits. In addition, players use several mnemonic tricks, such as planning in advance the kind of opening they play on a given board, and making associations between the face or the voice of the opponents and the game itself.

The current world record is a staggering 48 games, established in 2016 in Las Vegas by Uzbek grandmaster Timur Gareyev, who beat the record held by German master Marc Lang by two games. During the entire exhibition, Gareyev wore a blindfold mask and pedalled on an exercise bike, which he found useful to keep relaxed and focused. After 19 hours and 9 minutes – which included a 30-minute break due to a fire alarm! – and about 1,400 moves, he obtained a result of 35 wins, 7 draws and 6 losses, thus scoring 80.2% of the points. (He also rode more than 80 km!) Gareyev prepared for this event for several months. He used a variety of mnemonics including the "memory palace", where visual and conceptual associations are made with a list of pre-learnt locations, and the construction of connections using characteristics of the game, the board number and the name of the player. In an interview, he gave the examples of playing a risky opening on board 13 to try his luck and of associating the capture of a piece with a burst.

Starting in 1894 with Alfred Binet, the inventor of intelligence tests, there have been many informal accounts of blindfold chess in the literature. Reuben Fine, a world-class grandmaster who later became a psychoanalyst (see chapters 5 and 10) provided an interesting introspective account in a paper written in 1965. According to him, chess knowledge is essential. In particular, strong players use hierarchical "spatio-temporal Gestalts" that make it possible to understand the position as a whole. Although Fine was one of the few players who also stressed the capacity to visualise the board clearly, he also mentioned that pieces are perceived dynamically, not just as static objects. Additionally, he stressed the importance of using key statements for summing up positions (e.g. "a Sicilian defence, Taimanov variation, badly played by Black who has very weak dark squares").

A fair amount of research has been performed on blindfold chess. For example, Finnish psychologist Pertti Saariluoma carried out several fascinating experiments where he combined blindfold play with manipulations of memory load. Moves from a game were dictated at the pace of one per second. After 15 and 25 moves, players had to indicate the location of each piece. To spice things up, players had to perform an interfering task during the presentation of the game. This task was either verbal (to repeat the syllable "tik") or visuo-spatial (to form a mental image of three capital letters and mentally walk along the sides of these letters, saying whether the turns are left or right). There was also a control condition without any interfering task. The results showed that the visuo-spatial, but not the verbal task, had a negative effect on the performance in blindfold chess. In another experiment, the interfering tasks were given *after* the sequence of moves had been dictated. There was no loss in performance in either condition. Based on these and other experiments, Saariluoma concluded that blindfold chess requires visuo-spatial working memory but not verbal working memory. He also inferred that, more than differences in imagery ability, knowledge is the essential ingredient of blindfold chess, and specifically knowledge coded as chunks linked to possible actions.

Blindfold chess raises an interesting paradox. If strong players are able to play a game without seeing the board – as grandmasters clearly do – why is it that they do not do it in normal games? Surely, staring at the board in front of them creates serious interferences with the positions that they imagine in their mind's eye during look-ahead search. In fact, some players such as Ukrainian grandmaster Vassily Ivanchuk occasionally do so. The reason that most players do not do it can probably be explained by the fact that the physical chessboard provides visuo-spatial information that supplies memory support for the location of pieces. Still, as we shall see in Chapter 7, there are well-documented cases were players made errors in their calculations because they thought a piece was still on the square it was located on the external board, and not on the square it had moved to during look-ahead search.

3

THE BEST MOVE

The previous two chapters have provided considerable evidence for the role of perception and knowledge in chess. But obviously, chess players must be doing something else than just recognising good moves automatically. Else, why do they not play immediately, rather than pondering about their next move, sometimes for very long periods of time? For example, in the 14th game of the world championship match in Merano in 1981, Korchnoi thought for 1 hour and 20 minutes on his 13th move before moving his bishop one square up in reply to Karpov's knight's move.

The beauty of chess is that the number of possibilities grows extremely rapidly. There are about 35 legal moves in a middle game position, on average. Anticipating all possibilities two moves ahead requires considering 35×35 moves $= 35^2 = 1,225$ moves. The number of legal continuations six moves deep already reaches $35^6 = 1.83$ billion. Obviously, numbers keep increasing exponentially for greater depths. No player can carry out a systematic search – not even Korchnoi in 1 hour and 20 minutes! – except for trivial positions.

As pointed out by de Groot, look-ahead search must be highly selective and informed by chess knowledge. In his experiment, even world-class players rarely considered more than 100 possible continuations before making their move. But how do players carry out their search? Do they sometimes search very deeply? What kind of knowledge do they use? This chapter will answer these questions.

DE GROOT'S SURPRISING RESULTS

Again, the starting point is de Groot's PhD thesis. It aimed to understand how chess players think, and in particular what are the differences between strong players – masters and grandmasters – and weaker players. The chess literature offered two contradictory views. The majority of the authors argued that the ability of looking ahead was central to chess expertise, often referring to the deep combinations dreamt up by world champion Alexander Alekhine. Others argued that selectivity was key. When asked how many moves he normally saw ahead, grandmaster Richard Réti, one of the best players in the 1920s, is said to have replied: "Only one move, but the best one!"

As we have seen in Chapter 1, de Groot used a simple experimental procedure. He showed participants a chess position, and asked them to select their next move, as if they were playing one of their own games. This is a very common task for chess players, who also do this when they practice. In addition, de Groot asked them to think aloud. Again, this is not uncommon for chess players, who are used to talking together about their games and analysing moves. As there were no video recorders or smart phones at the time, de Groot would jot down on paper what the players said, and then clean up his notes. His sample was extraordinary, with six world-class players, including world champions Max Euwe and Alexander Alekhine. In addition, the sample included four Dutch masters, five candidate masters, two female Dutch champions and five weaker players.

NO SKILL DIFFERENCES IN THE STATISTICS OF SEARCH

As expected, grandmasters and masters selected better moves than weaker players. To understand how this difference came about, de Groot analysed the verbal protocols produced by the players both quantitatively and qualitatively. Nowadays, only the quantitative analyses are remembered in the scientific literature, which is a pity, as the more interpretative analyses tell us a lot about the cognitive processes underpinning chess players' thinking.

A protocol looks like this, omitting the chess notation:

> Great position. I have a strong attack. I have three possible moves: I can take her rook, retreat my rook or attack her queen with my knight. If I take her rook, she takes back, I can either give check with my bishop or attack her queen with my knight. In both cases, I'm winning. But she can also simply move her king, this is very annoying. So, in my first move, I can also retreat my rook. I don't like this. I can also attack her queen with my knight. She must move her queen here and then I give check with my bishop. It's winning. Let's calculate again. I attack her queen, she goes here, and I give check. OK, I play this move.

A player's thoughts can be displayed by a search tree (see Figure 3.1). Each node represents a position, and the moves are indicated on the branches. This representation makes it easy to compute

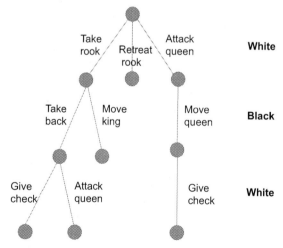

Figure 3.1 Example of a search tree.

measures such as the number of different moves considered (nine in the example) and the maximal depth of search (three moves).

The quantitative analyses focused on the differences between grandmasters and candidate masters. De Groot devised about 15 measures, including the time to make a decision, the number of different first moves considered, the number of different positions explored during search and the average depth of search. To de Groot's surprise, grandmasters and candidate masters did not differ with respect to the majority of these variables. In particular, depth of search was about the same between the two groups. In addition, all players were highly selective; out of about 30 possible first moves for White in the problem position, players considered only about three or four of them. Even when differences were found, such as with the rate of generating moves, they were small and insufficient to explain the large disparity in the quality of moves chosen.

PROGRESSIVE DEEPENING

The qualitative analyses describe, in great detail, the way the decision processes are structured. Most of de Groot's book is devoted to them. An important outcome was that all players were investigating the same base move (one of the first moves in the problem situation) several times – a process that de Groot called *progressive deepening*. The reinvestigation could be immediate, or separated by the analysis of another base move. In either case, reinvestigating a base move makes it possible for the player to study it with more precision, by increasing the number of moves anticipated or by improving the evaluation of the terminal position.

At first blush, this process seems repetitive and inefficient, since one might think that resources could be better used by analysing different base moves and new sequences of moves. However, progressive deepening is actually quite adaptive. First, it helps alleviate the restrictions imposed by the limited capacity of short-term memory. Revisiting the same sequence of moves several times increases the likelihood that it is stored in long-term memory, thus making analysis easier as more cognitive resources can be expended on it. Second, it makes it possible for players to use information that has been gleaned at different places of the search tree.

Finally, progressive deepening reflects the cyclic organisation of chess players' thought, which consists of several observation-test-evaluation phases. Anticipating ideas later developed by Newell and Simon during the cognitive revolution in psychology, de Groot proposed that the thoughts of a chess player can be described as complex hierarchies of problems and sub-problems. To deal with sub-problems, larger cycles may include smaller cycles. For de Groot, progressive deepening is not unique to chess, but is a fundamental characteristic of the way humans tackle complex problems and make decisions. As a paradigmatic example of this, de Groot mentions scientific research, where a researcher explores one possible solution, then examines another one, then goes back to the first solution and so on. In science, this process can take minutes, hours, days or even years.

THE PHASES OF CHESS THINKING

According to de Groot, chess players' thinking is typically divided into four phases: orientation, exploration, investigation and proof. During the orientation phase, players gather relevant information and provide a first preliminary evaluation of the position. This is followed by the exploration phase, where players analyse sample variations and progressively reduce the number of critical moves to two. These two moves are carefully examined during the investigation phase, where search is carried out at a deeper level than during the exploration phase. During this phase, players also try to find support for their favourite move. Interestingly, most of the arguments deployed by chess players are really an attempt to convince themselves that one of the two moves they had selected is better than the other. The final phase, called the proof phase, sees players recapitulate the conclusions obtained in the previous phase and double-check that the argumentation is correct.

As we have seen in the previous chapter, players rely on a great deal of knowledge, which includes strategic goals and plans, tactical motifs, specific methods for converting a material advantage and so on. There are vast skill and individual differences in the extent and use of this knowledge, which is domain specific (i.e. limited to chess).

MACROSTRUCTURE OF SEARCH: THERE ARE SKILL DIFFERENCES!

While most of de Groot's conclusions were insightful, there was ample space for further research to expand our understanding of chess players' thinking. Remember that de Groot found only very few skill differences with respect to the quantitative variables describing search. However, one should not forget that he compared grandmasters with candidate masters, who are fairly experienced players. In fact, when later researchers included weaker players in their sample, a number of differences became apparent. At the extreme, most beginners do not have the ability of anticipating any moves in their mind's eye, and thus the difference between grandmasters and novices is considerable. Differences remain when more experienced amateurs are considered, although these differences are not particularly large. For example, depth of search increases rapidly in the early stages of expertise, but improvement then becomes slower and slower; this kind of improvement, called the "power law of learning", is common in the literature of skill acquisition. With a power law, it is hard to detect skill differences with highly skilled players, since differences rapidly become minuscule. The data show that, on average, class D players search 2.3 moves deep, candidate masters 4.8 moves deep, and top-level grandmasters 5.3 moves deep. The last two data points are from de Groot's seminal study, and the difference is not large enough to detect statistically with a small sample.

Most statistics in de Groot's study were collected with a relatively simple position. When unfamiliar, complex and tactical positions are used, the skill differences in search increase considerably. For example, in a study carried out with Guillermo Campitelli, we chose "crazy" positions where the best moves were very difficult to find. The grandmaster had an average search of 13.8 moves, with some lines being searched 25 moves deep. The corresponding numbers for the class B player were 2.8 moves and 10.5 moves – a huge difference! Thus, strong players can adapt their search strategy to different kinds of positions, while this is not possible for weaker players. This seems to suggest that experts are more flexible with their use of search strategies than non-experts.

Another interesting result is that there are skill differences with respect to progressive deepening. A branch in the search tree can be re-examined in two different ways: either directly after (*immediate reinvestigation*), or after having examined one or several other branches (*non-immediate reinvestigation*). Re-analysing data I had collected as an undergraduate student, I found that stronger players tend to use more immediate reinvestigations and fewer non-immediate reinvestigations than weaker players. Strong players seem to use a *win-stay* and *lose-shift* strategy, to use terms from game theory. If the evaluation of a sequence of moves is positive, they search it again at a deeper level, verifying that the opponent does not have any moves that refute it. If the evaluation is negative, they consider the line as unfavourable and examine other moves, widening their search. In most positions, strong players rapidly identify promising moves by pattern recognition (see Chapter 2) and thus are likely to stay with them rather than considering other moves.

JUDGEMENT AND PLANNING

Judgement and Planning in Chess, written in 1952, is a famous book for intermediate-level players, in which world champion Max Euwe provides advice about topics such as weak pawns, strong squares and the pawn majority on the queenside. Judgement and planning are indeed two central concepts in chess, and Euwe's book is only one of the many treatises in the practical chess literature advising players how to excel in such skills. Judgement concerns the evaluation of the position. Do I have the advantage? What are my strengths and weaknesses, and those of my opponent? In a very old paper (1907!), Cleveland reports the results of a questionnaire that clearly show that stronger players evaluate positions better. More surprising is the observation made by de Groot in his thesis that evaluations typically concern only one aspect of the position, and more rarely two or three. For example: "Black is better because White's square f3 is very weak". There are actually also many instances in his protocols where players provide only broad evaluations such as "Black is better", without any supporting reason.

The way humans evaluate chess positions is a very far cry from the way computers do it, putting together dozens of factors such as control of the centre, piece mobility, material balance and king safety. It is as if players first evaluate the position unconsciously and automatically, presumably by pattern recognition, and then come up with one or two features to justify their evaluation. Obviously, this is not consistent with full rationality, according to which all the features of the position should be combined mathematically in the computation of the evaluation function, just as is done by computers.

In the late 1970s, Dennis Holding carried out several experiments in order to understand how chess players judge positions. In one experiment, he estimated the quality of players' evaluations as a function of depth of search. A computer programme provided an estimation of the correct evaluation. In general, stronger players provided better evaluations than weaker players, and the best evaluations were for the positions as they were on the external board. In addition, as the positions imagined during look-ahead search went deeper in the search tree, and thus farther from the problem situation, the quality of the evaluations went down. Another interesting result was that better players were more discriminative than weaker players in their judgements, giving high scores to positions where they had a clear advantage, and low scores to positions where the opponent had a clear advantage. By contrast, the weaker players tended to think that both sides had about equal chances, even when this was not the case.

Planning is the setting of long-term goals and the way to achieve them. Unlike the type of search I have discussed so far, which is typically move by move, planning omits many details and often does not include specific moves. We know from anecdotal evidence that strong players are good at finding a correct plan. Indeed, as already noted by de Groot, strong players often perceive the correct plan in a few seconds, just by recognising the type of position they are facing and retrieving similar situations from their long-term memory. This is often an instance of case-based reasoning: this position reminds me of the game X vs. Y, thus the plan should be first A, then B and finally C. At least in typical positions, plans are retrieved without any look-ahead search or even any explicit evaluation of the position. Of course, when the tactics turn out unfavourably, there might be a need to find a new plan. For example, from the original plan of attacking the opponent's king, one has to satisfy oneself with the less glorious plan of defending a weak pawn. Somewhat surprisingly, there is not much scientific research on planning in chess.

SCHEMAS AND MIND SETS

As seen in the previous chapter, de Groot highlighted the role of schematic knowledge in perception and problem-solving. Much of this knowledge is reproductive, which means that players, when possible, tend to choose stereotypical but efficient solutions over creative solutions. This knowledge enables masters to play good chess without much search or thinking, simply by applying known methods and principles. Experiments carried out by Pertti Saariluoma as well as Merim Bilalić and colleagues have buttressed this hypothesis. When presented with problems with stereotypical solutions, players tend to find these solutions, even when shorter but more original solutions are present. Does this mean that players become more rigid as their expertise increases?

In a series of clever experiments, Bilalić and colleagues showed that this is not the case. They induced mind-set effects (also known as Einstellung effects) by creating problems that had two solutions: a familiar but longer solution and an unfamiliar but shorter solution. Not only did players spot the familiar solution rapidly, but they could not find the shorter solution when requested to do so. It is not that the shorter solution was particularly hard. It was found rapidly by a control group who saw slightly modified positions so that only the shorter solution was possible. The mind-set effects were present even with candidate masters and masters. However, the crucial result was that these effects became weaker as the strength of the players increased. Thus, the more expert players were *less* rigid than the less expert players.

Mind-set effects pervade human cognition, as for example can be seen with racist and sexist stereotypes in social psychology and confirmation bias in cognitive psychology. Be it in politics, science or relationships, people tend to select information that supports their views and ignore information that challenges them. Could chess shed light on the mechanisms that underpin these mind-set effects? Bilalić and colleagues recorded the eye movements of candidate masters confronted with the type of two-solution problems discussed above. As in previous experiments, players found the stereotypical solution rapidly and failed to find the short solution. Here comes the fascinating part of the results: all players said they looked at other moves and tried hard to find the shorter solution. However, their eye movements told a different story: players kept looking at the squares critical for the stereotypical solution, even though they thought that they were looking at other parts of the board. It is as if, once a schema linked to the familiar solution had been activated by perceptual patterns on the board, players could not inhibit it. Beyond chess, these results raise profound and troubling questions about introspection, consciousness and free will.

PLAYING AGAINST KASPAROV

This chapter has shown that there is considerable evidence for the importance of search in chess decision-making. Similarly, the previous two chapters have documented the great significance of pattern recognition. There has been much debate in psychology about the respective roles of these two mechanisms. Whilst de Groot and Simon emphasised the roles of perception and knowledge, they also agreed that look-ahead search was important. However, they both stressed that search was highly selective (rarely more than 100 positions), precisely because of the knowledge that players can bring to bear. In addition, Simon repeatedly pointed out that search must be limited because of the constraints imposed by the limited capacity of short-term memory and the bottleneck of attention.

There is also substantial empirical evidence for pattern recognition. To begin with, support is offered by strong players' ability to zoom in rapidly on promising moves, as already documented by de Groot and later corroborated by more experimental research. Then, there is the fact that grandmasters maintain a fairly high quality of play when they compete in speed chess tournaments, where they have about 5 seconds per move – a drastic reduction in comparison to standard games (2–3 minutes per move). Finally, compelling evidence is provided by simultaneous displays, where one player (typically a master or a grandmaster) plays against 20 or 30 amateurs. These exhibitions are spectacular, not least because the master typically wins most games, in spite of spending only a few seconds on each move. In fact, simultaneous games are tough not because of the difficulty of the games – the difference in expertise is such that playing normal moves and waiting for the opponent to make a mistake is normally sufficient for winning a game – but because the master must walk several kilometres in the process!

Perhaps the most arresting example of simultaneous chess was offered by world champion Garry Kasparov, who played against entire national teams! For example, in 1992 he beat the German team, which consisted of four seasoned grandmasters, by the score of 3 to 1. Simon and I used the results of seven such matches and two matches against the team of Hamburg to argue that knowledge, accessed by pattern recognition, plays a larger part in chess expertise than does anticipating moves ahead. Unlike standard simultaneous displays, where the master always has White and thus enjoys a small starting advantage in all the games, in these matches Kasparov had White in half of the games and Black in the other half. Out of the nine matches he had played at the time, Kasparov won eight of them; he lost only his first match, presumably because he was new to this type of event. His median performance was 2646 Elo, which was the strength of a top grandmaster at the time and would still have placed him in the best six players in the world. In fact, Kasparov's performance in these matches was typically less than 100 points below the level displayed in normal tournament play. For example, his rating in July 1987 was 2735.

The teams consisted of four to eight strong masters and grandmasters, and thus Kasparov's thinking time was reduced proportionally. As search is carried out serially and relatively slowly (perhaps 10 positions per minute, based on de Groot's data), reducing thinking time should affect the number of positions examined and consequently decrease performance. The loss should not be as large if pattern recognition played a larger role, because this process is assumed to occur rapidly. That is what was observed in the actual results. In line with this analysis, there was no correlation between Kasparov's performance and the number of opponents he was facing, which directly affected the time available for his thinking.

While I still believe that this analysis is correct, two factors should be taken into account. The first is that Kasparov did carry out a fair amount of search, as is obvious from looking at the games he played in these matches. The opposition essentially consisted of professional players, including many grandmasters; therefore, he could not just play normal moves and wait for the opponent to make a mistake. He had to provoke such mistakes by complicating games, which he did with brio. The second factor, related to the first, is that Kasparov was extremely well prepared for these encounters, with the exception of the first one, as noted above. He would analyse at least 100 games of each of his opponents to identify their strengths and weaknesses. Then, he would use this knowledge to steer the play into the kind of positions that a specific opponent did not handle well and thus increase the chances for that opponent to play inferior moves. For example, if an opponent was relatively weak in anticipating a sudden attack in what seems a quiet strategic position, Kasparov would choose an opening likely to lead to such a position, even if this meant a slight disadvantage. In addition to creating positions where his opponents could not play at their best, this approach also had the advantage of reducing the search space, as some moves would not even be considered if they did not fit Kasparov's plan. Obviously, it could be argued that his opponents could have used the same stratagem, studying Kasparov's games to take advantage of his weaknesses. The problem, however, is not only that Kasparov had far fewer weaknesses, but also that his opponents in general did not have sufficient mastery of chess to implement such a plan.

It turns out that I played against Kasparov when he took on the six-man Swiss national team, which was held in 1987 in Zurich. Playing White, I entered a variation that he had prepared for the world championship match against Anatoly Karpov. There was a possibility for me to conclude the game with an early draw, by repeating the same position three times. However, as a team we had agreed not to accept such early draw offers, which would have made Kasparov's task easier, and I kept playing. With hindsight, this was a mistake, as I rapidly lost my bearings in wild tactical complications and got roundly beaten. In a sense, there was no game, as all the key moves had been anticipated in Kasparov's home preparation. The other five games were more balanced but Switzerland got smashed 5½ – ½.

Even more impressive than the match results were the post-mortem analyses. To begin with, the analysis that Kasparov made of our strengths and (mostly) weaknesses were spot on. After analysing 100 of our games, he had a better understanding than we had of the play of our teammates, whom we had known for many years, and even of our own play. In several games, he fully implemented his plan, including the example I gave earlier of a player having a poor sense of danger in quiet positions. In fact, in spite of theoretically having six times less time for calculating variations than his opponents, he actually calculated deeper and better. The impression was that he was able to generate the first moves of the key variations quickly – presumably by using his knowledge of typical sequences of moves in similar positions – and really started computing moves at the point where we had to stop because we had reached the limit of our look-ahead capability. In 1986, leading British grandmaster Anthony Miles, after losing a match against Kasparov 5½ – ½, called him "a monster with a hundred eyes who sees everything". We came to appreciate how appropriate this description was. Incidentally, that day I understood that I should spend more time studying for my PhD in psychology and less on chess!

4

PRACTICE MAKES (ALMOST) PERFECT

Can anybody be a grandmaster in chess through hard practice, or is some special talent needed? This is the classical nature vs. nurture question, which still pervades psychology, polarising research. The nature side claims that innate talent is needed. The idea goes back to polymath Francis Galton, a cousin of Charles Darwin, who among other things invented fingerprinting for identifying humans. Comparing the pedigree of natural sons of eminent men with adoptive sons of the same men, he concluded that eminence is hereditary. By contrast, the nurture side of the argument rejects any role for talent and contends that practice is all that is needed. One of the major proponents of this idea was John Watson, the father of behaviourism. In his 1930 book *Behaviorism*, he made his point of view crystal clear:

> Give me a dozen healthy infants, well-formed, and my own speci-
> fied world to bring them up in and I'll guarantee to take any
> one at random and train him to become any type of specialist
> I might select – doctor, lawyer, artist, merchant-chief and, yes,
> even beggar-man and thief, regardless of his talents, penchants,
> tendencies, abilities, vocations and race of his ancestors.

In spite of more than a century of arguments, the debate still rages. One reason behind the popularity of this question is that the way one answers it has huge implications for education and training, not only in schools but also in business and industry. Common sense would argue that both talent and practice matter, but researchers sometimes lack common sense! Indeed, they are still taking rather extreme positions nowadays. For example, in a famous paper emphasising the role of deliberate practice, Anders Ericsson and colleagues argued that, with the right kind of practice, anybody can reach the highest levels of expertise. At the other extreme, British psychologist Hans Eysenck argued that, unless one is talented, there is no hope of reaching high levels in a domain. As it turns out, research on chess has much to say on this question.

THE CASE FOR PRACTICE

Currently, the pendulum has swung to the practice side, in particular due to the popularity of the deliberate practice framework, developed in 1993 by Anders Ericsson, Ralf Krampe and Clemens Tesch-Römer. The central idea is that talent is not necessary to reach superior performance, but that the right kind of practice – called deliberate practice – is sufficient. Such practice is characterised by activities aiming to improve performance. These activities, which tend to be carried out solitarily, aim to correct errors and improve weaknesses by using rapid and informative feedback. They must be carried out for many years, and are effortful, not enjoyable. They also require concentration and thus can be done only for a few hours a day. In addition, they require the presence of a coach, and, in some domains such as figure skating or swimming, access to expensive sport facilities. Therefore, deliberate practice is possible only when there is a suitable environment, including strong financial and family support. Ericsson and colleagues emphasise both the quality and the amount of practice and argue that, in nearly all domains of expertise, at least 10 years, or 10,000 hours, of practice are necessary for reaching top levels. They report data from classical pianists and violinists, but make it clear that their conclusions apply to any domain of expertise. The role of talent is rejected, except for height, motivation and the capacity to engage in deliberate practice. Importantly for our discussion of chess skill, the authors argue that expert performance does not depend on inherited cognitive abilities.

These ideas are certainly reasonable from chess players' point of view. Many players have the reputation of working extremely hard to improve or maintain their skill level. Hungarian grandmaster Lajos Portisch was known to analyse games eight hours a day, every day. World champions Bobby Fischer and Magnus Carlsen said in interviews that they think about chess nearly all the time. A biography of the three Polgár sisters mentioned that they practiced from 8 to 10 hours a day. These ideas are also consistent with what I have said about the importance of chunking and knowledge in becoming a chess expert. If players must acquire a large number of chunks to reach high levels of skill, then it stands to reason that they will have to devote considerable amounts of time to study and practice chess.

Another line of support for the role of practice in chess stems from the fact that players' overall skill level has massively increased following four innovations in the way chess knowledge is transmitted. First, in the 1960s, a group of Belgrade masters and grandmasters started publishing the *Chess Informant*, a book originally published twice a year (and now four times a year), which made widely available information that was before restricted to Soviet players. The great originality of the series was that it developed an international chess language that basically eliminated language barriers. Second, in the 1970s, the publication of the five-volume collection of the *Encyclopaedia of Chess Openings* systematised the theory of chess openings, the knowledge of which is central for becoming a strong player. Third, starting from the late 1980s, computerised chess databases and increasingly strong chess engines revolutionised training and tournament preparation. Earlier, even after the advent of the *Chess Informant* and the *Encyclopaedia of Chess Openings*, it was necessary to comb dozens of books and magazines to find the relevant information, and then to play the games on a physical chessboard, which was time consuming. Suddenly, hundreds of games could be accessed in an eye blink, and rapidly played on the computer screen. In addition, it became possible to use chess engines to analyse games and, in particular, to explore and test new ideas in the openings. Finally, the Internet made it possible to play chess 24 hours a day, seven days a week, against opponents that include many grandmasters.

Ericsson and colleagues made their case by collecting data on violinists and pianists of different levels of expertise. They also referred to chess several times, noting that no player, including Bobby Fischer, became grandmaster in less than 10 years of practice. Several empirical studies have tested Ericsson and colleagues' claims. In a first study led by Neil Charness, a colleague of Ericsson at the University of Tallahassee in Florida, chess players were asked about the type and duration of their practice activities. Overall, the results supported deliberate practice. There was a strong correlation between players' rating and the number of hours they had spent studying chess alone. This correlation was stronger than that between rating and the number of hours players had spent practicing or studying with others. They also found that the presence of a coach had no effect on skill, once the number of hours devoted to solitary practice was controlled for statistically. Interestingly, the number of books owned was a predictor beyond deliberate practice. Whether this result is still valid today is an interesting question. The data were collected in 1993 and 1994, and books were then the main means by which players acquired chess knowledge. As noted above, chess players' practice today consists of using databases storing millions of games, analysing games with computer programmes that are vastly stronger than world-class grandmasters and playing games on the Internet.

PRACTICE IS NOT ENOUGH

Together with my PhD student Guillermo Campitelli, I replicated Charness's study. Many of our findings were in line with the earlier study, but some were at variance with the deliberate practice framework. On the positive side, we found that players needed, on average, about 11,000 hours to become a master. In addition, deliberate practice explained about 18% of the variance in skill, which is not far from the 25% found by Charness and colleagues. On the negative side, several results did not fit the predictions of the theory at all. First, group practice, which included competitive games and practicing with other players, had a more important role than individual practice. Second, even though the (future) candidate masters and masters had practiced the same amount of time during the first three years of serious practice, the masters already had higher ratings at this stage. This counts against the hypothesis that skill is a monotonic function of the amount of deliberate practice. Third, the candidate masters did not improve much after these first three years in spite of considerable amounts of deliberate practice. Fourth, Ericsson and colleagues argued that the most important and frequent activity training activity was to predict the next move in masters' games, compare one's answer with the move actually played and receive immediate feedback. We found that players engaged in numerous other activities, such as studying openings and endgames, finding new moves in the opening to surprise their opponents and playing games against humans and computers.

Finally, and most importantly, there was a huge inter-individual variability in the amount of deliberate practice. The quickest players needed only 3,000 hours of deliberate practice to reach master level, while the slowest needed 24,000 hours – that is eight times longer, a huge difference! In addition, some players devoted more than 25,000 hours to deliberate practice, but never reached master level.

This inter-individual variability, which counts against the assumption that it takes 10 years to become an expert, is also reflected at the top level. While it is true that many players needed at least 10 years of dedicated practice to become grandmaster, others were much quicker. Sergey Karjakin holds the record of world's youngest grandmaster: he obtained the title at the age of 12 years, 7 months and 0 days, seven years after learning the rules. Current world champion Magnus Carlsen was even quicker: he started practicing chess at the age of 8 years and became grandmaster at the age of 13 years, 3 months and 27 days – that is, only five years and four months of deliberate practice! Carlsen is actually not known to be the most assiduous worker – for example, he prefers watching or playing football to studying chess. In a 2014 study with my PhD student Morgan Ereku, I estimated the amount of time that the top 11 players in the world had engaged in deliberate practice. We found that Carlsen's number of years of practice was significantly *less* than the average of the other players. In spite of this, the difference between Carlsen and the second player in the world (Levon Aronian) was 66 Elo points, which was about the same as the difference between Aronian and the 14th player in the world (Anish Giri)!

STARTING AGE, HANDEDNESS AND SEASONALITY OF BIRTH

A major weakness of this field of research is that nearly all studies have only used measures directly related to deliberate practice and did not consider other possible explanations for skilled behaviour. The study with Campitelli was an exception, as we also used several measures unrelated to deliberate practice. The results suggested that other factors are important in reaching high levels of expertise. To begin with, the age at which players started to practice chess seriously correlated with skill level, even after controlling for deliberate practice statistically. The younger the players started practicing chess seriously, the better they became. The effect was rather strong: players who started to play seriously at the age of 12 or before had 1 chance out of 4 to become an international-level player – not a bad deal! – but players who started to play after the age of 12 had only 2 chances out of 100 to reach that goal. The results supported the hypothesis that there is a critical period for acquiring chess skill, a hypothesis originally proposed by Arpad Elo, the creator of the Elo rating.

The second factor beyond practice that we investigated was handedness. Handedness is a classic marker of talent in domains such as music, mathematics and the visual arts. Our results showed a link between handedness and chess skill. Chess players tended to be more often left-handed or ambidextrous than the population at large (18% vs. 10.2%, respectively). Also, the degree of handedness was less extreme with chess players. That is, they tended to be more mixed-handed. However, when considering chess players only, there was no correlation between handedness and skill level.

Finally, together with another PhD student, Philippe Chassy, I found that there was a link between seasonality of birth and chess skill. Chess players in the northern hemisphere tend to be born more often in the first half of the year than in the second half. For players rated higher than 2000 points (candidate masters and above), the respective percentages were 52.3% and 47.7%; for players at the grandmaster level, the effect was stronger and the respective percentages were 56.9% and 43.1%.

There is a seasonal pattern in several sports as well (e.g. football players tend be born more often in the autumn). The standard explanation is selective drop-out, where younger children tend to leave the sport because they compete against peers who are a few months older and thus are on average stronger, faster and better coordinated. However, what is exciting about the chess data is that this explanation does not work: children playing chess compete against other children of varying ages and even against adults. What is then the explanation? A possibility is that the development of the foetus's brain is affected by external factors that tend to be present in late winter and early spring; the likely culprits are viruses, and in particular the flu virus. Remarkably, the same month-of-birth pattern has been found with schizophrenia, where a similar explanation has been proposed. Chapter 10 will discuss the possible link between chess and psychopathology.

TALENT IN CHESS

As noted at the beginning of this chapter, the main alternative explanation to practice is talent. Theoretically, there are good reasons to believe that there are innate differences in cognitive abilities in general, and in those underpinning chess skill in particular. From an evolutionary point of view, variability is necessary for evolving not only physical but also cognitive traits, as was already demonstrated by Charles Darwin in the 19th century. In addition, going back to chunking theory described in Chapter 2, it is reasonable to assume that there are individual differences with respect to its parameters. For example, one individual might need 8.5 seconds to learn a chunk, but another only 7.5 seconds. Given the vast number of chunks that must be learnt, even small differences could have huge effects after years of practice. Similarly, a larger short-term memory capacity would make it easier to learn chunks and other useful information. It would also facilitate real-time information processing, for example when carrying out look-ahead search. Finally, the hypothesis of individual differences in cognitive ability is clearly supported by the substantial literature on intelligence.

This hypothesis is also supported by child prodigies. In her PhD thesis, Yu-Hsuan Chang reports the case of an exceptional 10-year-old American female chess player, known only as CS, who needed little time to become an expert. It took her only about 160 hours of individual study and 3,800 hours of overall chess-related experience to reach a rating of 2141. Interestingly, CS scored much better than a control group on a test of visual short-term memory. The case of Canadian player Harmony Zhu is remarkable as well. She became world champion at age 7 in the Girls Under 8 Category. At 1545, her rating is not that impressive; however, this is more than compensated for by the fact that she is also an accomplished concert pianist. Before reaching the age of 11, she had played with several renowned orchestras, such as the Philadelphia Orchestra and the Israel Philharmonic Orchestra, and won numerous piano competitions. Chess and music do not always go along well together, however. "It bothers me so much", says Harmony, "that I can hardly concentrate on the chessboard because of my own composed music in my head!" In spite of her talents, she remains a normal child. Interviewed after winning the chess world title for her age, she was asked about her coach, but could not remember whether he was a grandmaster or even his name. Unfazed, she carried on: "Oh, oh by the way, you know I have a pet guinea pig? . . . And his name is Scrumptious. . . . He's a white guinea pig".

In recent years, the importance of talent in chess has received strong empirical support, mostly from research into intelligence but also from research into personality. While a fair amount of research had been carried out for a long time on the link between intelligence and chess, the results seemed conflicting. This was, for example, the conclusion I reached in my book *Understanding Expertise*, published just three years ago. However, two very recent meta-analyses, carried out by a group of researchers at the University of Liverpool and Michigan State University, and led by PhD students Alexander Burgoyne and Giovanni Sala, have shed important light on this apparent inconsistency. (A meta-analysis is a statistical technique putting together the results of all the studies that can be found on a particular topic. Meta-analyses make it possible to draw more reliable conclusions than single experiments, not only because they rely on a larger number of participants but also because studies are replicated several times, with different research groups and populations.)

The first study found that chess players were more intelligent, on average, than people who do not play chess. The effect size was half a standard deviation – a medium-size effect. The second study found that skill in chess correlated with different measures of intelligence, including fluid reasoning, short-term memory and processing speed. The highest correlation was with numerical ability (0.35) while, somewhat surprisingly, the correlation with visuo-spatial ability was only modest (0.13). On average, the correlations were about 0.25. Interestingly, the correlations were stronger with youth samples than with adult samples and with unranked players than with ranked players. As we shall see in Chapter 9, teaching individuals to play chess is unlikely to improve their intelligence, which rules out the possibility that there is a causal link from chess to intelligence. Thus, the results of the two meta-analyses suggest that individual differences in chess skill are in part caused by differences in cognitive ability, in particular with young chess players and weak players.

Given their high level of heritability, the presence of distinct personality traits in chess players would provide additional support for the presence of innate talent. A study with my PhD student Merim

Bilalić showed that children who play chess regularly tend to be more extroverted, more open to new experiences and more prone to arguing (as shown by their low scores on the measure of "agreeableness") than children who do not play chess. None of the measures correlated with skill level. In addition, boys obtained lower scores on agreeableness than girls, a finding that has been repeatedly obtained in adult samples. Given the competitive nature of chess, this result might suggest a reason why boys tend to be more interested in chess than girls. In another study by Sabine Vollstädt-Klein and colleagues, elite chess players filled in a personality inventory. It was found that the personality profile of male players did not differ from the population. By contrast, female players tended to have higher levels of satisfaction with life, to have fewer physical complaints and to display higher achievement motivation than the population. With males, stronger players tended to be more introvert, while, with females, the opposite was true. Stronger female players were also more aggressive.

INTERACTION BETWEEN PRACTICE AND TALENT IS KEY

While research in chess psychology, like other fields of psychology, has been highly polarised between the extreme positions of practice and talent, it is almost certain that the truth lies somewhere in the middle. Importantly, there will be important interactions between practice and talent, not only at a given point in time, but also as expertise develops. These ideas are captured in what could be called the "spaghetti model" (see Figure 4.1). In this model, the environment has an effect on practice, intelligence and performance; intelligence has an effect on practice and performance; finally, practice and performance mutually affect each other, perhaps because increasing one's performance boosts motivation and hence practice. A complete model is likely to be much more complicated – for example, personality and motivation should be included – but this model captures some of the main features of the development of chess skill.

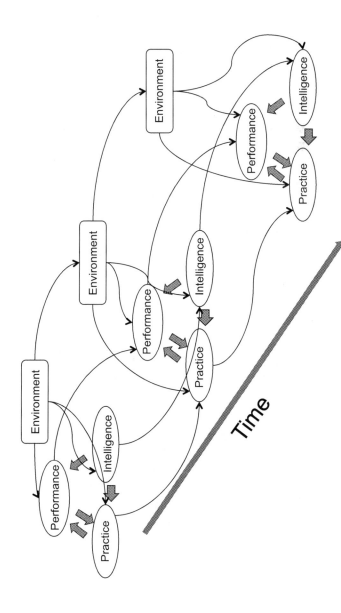

Figure 4.1 The spaghetti model, which emphasises interactions between environmental and innate factors.

An important aspect of the model is the presence of feedback loops. For example, intelligence affects both practice and performance, but in turn performance affects the amount and quality of practice. A second important aspect of the model is its dynamic nature, in the sense that it captures the time dimension. For example, practice at time 1 will affect practice at time 2. A third important aspect is that the model captures what is sometimes called the rich-get-richer effect, which also relates to chaos theory in mathematics: small changes at the beginning might amplify and have huge consequences much later. For example, let us go back to the hypothesis that individuals might differ with respect to the rate at which they learn a chunk. One person might have a rate of 7.9 seconds per chunk, another 8.1 seconds per chunk. The difference is small, but propagated over the acquisition of 100,000 chunks, the effects become considerable. In particular, the effects are amplified by other factors. For example, a person acquiring chunks a bit quicker will be better at chess than her friends, other things being equal. She will win more games, which will increase her motivation and thus the time she spends studying chess. This will increase her strength even further.

Similar snowball effects are likely to occur with personality factors that encourage study and training, or that give that small additional edge in a long and difficult game. Such effects can also be caused by acquired factors, such as better heuristics for making decisions or better techniques for learning. Obviously, some of this knowledge might be communicated by experienced coaches.

Finally, there is a topic that has been little studied scientifically in chess but that is nonetheless critical: passion. Passion is a combination of love and obsession for the game, competitiveness and rage to win. All top-level players and most strong players have it.

5

MEN VS. WOMEN

Women have historically been underrepresented in several fields such as science, the arts and business. For example, there are very few female mathematicians, and the same applies to classic composers. For every Nobel Prize won by a woman in chemistry, physics and physiology/medicine, there are 35 won by men. Similarly, males still dominate in occupations such as engineering. What are the reasons behind this large gender gap? Several explanations have been proposed, including biological differences, socio-cultural and educational factors and motivational causes. In spite of the societal importance of the topic and considerable research efforts, no agreement has been reached among researchers. As we shall see, chess sheds some important light on some of these explanations.

There is little doubt that men perform better at chess than women. In the international rating list, there is only one woman for every 17 men. Currently, only one woman belongs to the best 100 players: Chinese grandmaster Hou Yifan, ranked at the 64th place with a rating of 2680. Before her, the only woman to be able to compete with the very best male players was Hungarian grandmaster Judit Polgár, who was ranked number 8 in the world at the peak of her career.

THE POLGÁR SISTERS

In 1965, László Polgár, a Hungarian educational psychologist, was courting his future wife Klara, a foreign language teacher from Ukraine. Rather than writing poetry, László used his love letters to convince Klara of his educational views. His key argument was simple, and actually went directly back to John Watson: there is a genius in every healthy child, and with the correct method of education, parents can grow their child into a famous mathematician, musician or scientist. László wanted to test his theory, and thus wanted to find a woman that would marry him and have children with him. Klara agreed.

They had three girls: Susan, Sofia and Judit. As there was no boy, the experiment gained additional piquancy: to show that girls are not inferior intellectually to boys and can reach top levels of expertise. The eldest sister, Susan, was born in 1969. László originally wanted to run his experiment with mathematics, but switched to chess because Susan adored the chess pieces – they were toys for her. She began playing chess when she was 4 years old. A few months later, she won the Budapest Girls' Under-11 Championship, with a 100% score. Susan became the highest-rated female chess player in the world at the age of 15 and earned the grandmaster title seven years later.

The education of Susan, and later of her two sisters, consisted of chess training for about 9 hours a day. In addition, she learnt mathematics and several foreign languages. Originally, her parents had to fight against the Hungarian educational system, as home schooling was unheard of in a communist country. Chess players were not impressed either, and were reluctant to help. However, as Susan started getting impressive results, the family increasingly received support from leading Hungarian chess players. László continuously refined his training methods, and there is no doubt that Sofia and Judit (born in 1974 and 1976, respectively) benefitted from this.

By far the strongest of the three was Judit. She was the youngest grandmaster ever when she was awarded the title in 1991, at the age of 15 years, 4 months and 28 days old, improving on Bobby Fischer, who got the title at 15 years, 6 months and 1 day. At one point ranked 8th in the world, she has won games (in either classic or rapid chess) against many of the top players of the world, including Anatoly Karpov, Garry Kasparov and Magnus Carlsen.

Sofia did not reach as high a level as her sisters. In an interview, Susan noted that Sofia was the most talented of the three, but also the laziest. That being said, when Sofia was 14 years old, she won a tournament in Rome ahead of several leading grandmasters, with the stunning score of 8½ out of 9 and a performance of 2879 Elo, which was at the time one of the highest in chess history.

The Polgár sisters also obtained remarkable results when playing together for Hungary, which might be called Polgáry, as they made up 75% of the four-player team. They won the women's chess Olympiads in 1988 and 1990, breaking a long series of victories by the Soviet Union.

László Polgár's experiment yielded clear results: his method of education, which emphasises specialising in a field from an early age, produced top-level chess players. But does it really prove that nurture is more important than nature? No, because the design of the experiment lacks a key feature: random selection of the participants. Thus, genetic influences are possible, even likely: László and Klara each have a PhD degree in education. A better design would be to raise randomly selected children. In fact, Dutch billionaire Joop van Oosterom proposed to do just this: he suggested to László and Klara Polgár that they could use their training methods with children from a developing country. László was interested, but Klara declined, probably wisely. As Susan Polgar put it in a *Psychology Today* interview: "[My mother] understood that life is not only about chess, and that all the rest would fall on her lap".

EXPLANATIONS

Gender differences in chess performance are not disputable. But what are the reasons? Are they the same as those proposed to explain gender differences in science, technology, engineering and mathematics

(STEM)? I briefly discuss five explanations: statistical, biological, socio-cultural, psychoanalytical and motivational.

Statistical explanations and participation rates

A first important statistical fact is that with intelligence and mathematics tests, males display greater variability than females. That is, the standard deviation is higher for male than female scores. Thus, extreme values are statistically more likely with males than females. So, with respect to intelligence, males are more likely to score either very high or very low. A 2006 study by Chabris and Glickman shows that this result does not hold for chess, since females' standard deviation was actually larger than males'. A second important statistical fact is that there are much fewer female than male players (as seen earlier, a 1:17 ratio in the international rating list). Thus, before we discuss other factors, we must consider the following simple statistical explanation: when there are two groups of different sizes, the best (and the worst) individuals are probabilistically more likely to come from the larger group. Bilalić and colleagues showed that this explanation successfully accounts for the gender differences in the German rating list. However, this is only part of the explanation, as the issue seems to be postponed: why do more boys than girls decide to play chess regularly?

Biological explanations

These are the preferred explanations by leading grandmasters. There are two main variants, both based on partly innate traits: the first is based on intelligence, the second on differences in aggressive behaviour. For example, in a 1962 interview Bobby Fischer put it bluntly: "They're all weak, all women. They're stupid compared to men. They shouldn't play chess, you know". In 1989, in an interview with *Playboy* magazine, Garry Kasparov was hardly more positive: "Well, in the past, I have said that there is real chess and women's chess. Some people don't like to hear this, but chess does not fit women properly. It's a fight, you know? A big fight. It's not for women. Sorry".

While the phrasing was unfortunate, Fischer and Kasparov have a point: there are gender differences with respect to intelligence and aggressiveness, as discussed in a massive scientific literature. But the story is more complicated than just males being more intelligent and more aggressive. In fact, most researchers agree that there are no gender differences with respect to overall or general intelligence. However, there are some more subtle differences, in particular when one considers particular cognitive abilities. Specifically, males do better on spatial tasks; for example, they perform nearly one standard deviation better in mental-rotation tasks. They also perform better in mechanical tests. By contrast, females do better with respect to face recognition, episodic memory tasks and language. For example, girls start talking sooner than boys and already have a larger vocabulary by the age of 3 years.

Gender differences in aggressiveness have been well-documented in psychology. On average, men are more aggressive than women. Men's aggressive behaviour tends to include direct aggression leading to physical pain and injury, while women tend to produce more indirect aggression such as psychological and social damage, for example by gossiping or spreading rumours. Men tend to use aggression as a means to exert control over other people, while women use aggression as a means to cope with extreme stress and loss of self-control. Gender differences occur early in childhood; for example, boys prefer violent games, while girls are attracted by educational and entertainment games.

There is much controversy about the reasons explaining gender differences in intelligence and aggressiveness. Some researchers have proposed that gender-specific evolutionary pressures have led to genetic differences affecting not only brain anatomy and physiology but also behaviour. Others have emphasised environmental factors, such as socialisation and the kind of toys and games given to girls and boys.

To my knowledge, the only study to have reported data on gender differences and intelligence with chess players is the study published in 2006 by Bilalić and colleagues. In their relatively small sample (57 children), boys performed better both in a chess test and an intelligence test. Another study by Bilalić and colleagues, already mentioned in Chapter 4, supported the hypothesis that boys are more aggressive than girls: in their sample, boys scored lower on agreeableness than girls. In addition, chess players scored lower than children who did not play chess.

Socio-cultural explanations

A standard explanation for gender differences in STEM disciplines and business is sexism and what is sometimes called the glass ceiling: an invisible but unbreakable barrier that makes it impossible for women and other minorities to progress to the highest levels of their field. Whether this explanation applies to chess is an interesting question. On the one hand, chess competitions are fair and open to anybody, assuming one has the required skill level. On the other hand, discrimination may be subtler. For example, the kind of comments made by Fischer and Kasparov certainly do not look like a welcoming message to women, nor does the fact that there are typically very few women in chess clubs.

Another socio-cultural explanation is that women, to some extent, are victims of an inferiority complex. They believe than men are better, perhaps because they think that chess corresponds to the type of intelligence (e.g. spatial and mathematical intelligence) that society assigns to males. When they face men, they may have smaller expectations and assume that they are weaker, and tend to confirm this prediction by losing more often than should be the case based on chess skill only. A variant of this hypothesis is stereotype threat, where the awareness of a negative stereotype negatively affects one's performance.

This hypothesis has received mixed support. In an experiment on stereotype threat carried out by Anne Maass and colleagues, participants played against an opponent via a computer. There were three conditions: (a) control group, with no knowledge of the opponent's gender; (b) high gender stereotype, where participants were told the opponent was a man; and (c) low gender stereotype, where participants were told that the opponent was a woman. In the last two conditions, the gender stereotype was made explicit by telling players that men play better chess than women. Women performed worse than men in the high stereotype condition, but not in the other two conditions. However, the hypothesis of stereotype threat was not supported in another study. In an analysis of over 5.5 million competitive games in international tournaments, Tom Stafford did not find any support for the stereotype threat hypothesis. Contrary to expectation, women actually performed better against men than expected from their ratings.

Psychoanalytical explanations

This is perhaps the less likely explanation, but it is worth discussing in some detail, as it has been widely publicised. For example, it was discussed in detail by grandmaster Reuben Fine, who, before becoming a Freudian psychoanalyst, was one of the contenders to the world championship title. (When Fine decided to leave chess to become a psychoanalyst, a fellow grandmaster joked: "a great loss to chess, and at best a draw for psychoanalysis".)

The theory, originally proposed by Ernest Jones, Sigmund Freud's official biographer, aimed to explain two sets of data: first, there are few female chess players, and second, several top-level players suffered from psychiatric disorders (see Chapter 10). According to the theory, women play badly because they do not want to play well! Chess is a substitute for war, and is characterised by anal-sadistic features. The familial constellation is symbolically reflected in chess: the father is the king, the mother is the queen and the child is the pawn. Thus, chess embodies the Oedipus complex. The male child wants to kill the father ("checkmate" means "the king is dead" in Persian) to seduce the mother. However, if the child is a girl, she wants to get rid of the mother to seduce the father. Therefore, there is no interest for a girl to checkmate the king, hence to kill him, since it is precisely he who is the subject of her seduction. As a consequence, women do not excel in chess. According to Freudian logic, the women who *do* excel in chess have a reverse Oedipus, where the girl sides with her mother to kill the father.

The theory has received little empirical support. For example, no systematic survey has tried to test Jones and Fine's hypotheses. Krogius, in his book the *Psychology in Chess*, notes that Freudian assumptions are "hard to believe" and regrets that Fine did not use his experience as a top-level grandmaster. I certainly agree with this evaluation. One could also mention that the idea of a reverse Oedipus is actually a clear example of an ad-hoc explanation to save a theory.

Motivational explanation: women have broader interests

A final explanation is that chess-playing women have broader interests than men. For example, they yearn for a recognised job, social and family life, and even spiritual development. Therefore, they are less likely to be obsessed by a single activity such as chess. This explanation is supported not only by interviews given by top female players, but also by their actual career choices.

Examples abound. Former world champion Maia Chiburdanidze studied medicine and engaged herself in social work. Grandmaster Dana Reizniece-Ozola, who represented Latvia several times in the Chess Olympiads, gave up chess to become Minister of Finance of her country. Hou Yifan, who became the women's world champion at the age of 14 and is currently the only woman to successfully compete with the best male players, studied international relations at Peking University, to the great despair of her coach. According to her, "chess is just a game; chess is not life". In 2018, she won a prestigious Rhodes Scholarship to study for an MSc in Education at the University of Oxford. To be clear, the highly competitive scholarship was awarded based on her academic performance and not her chess career. Previous well-known Rhodes Scholars include former US president Bill Clinton and former US National Security Advisor Susan Rice.

Some male players have, of course, also had careers beyond chess – good examples are Reuben Fine, whom I have discussed above, and

Kenneth Rogoff, an American grandmaster who became professor of economics at Harvard University and was chief economist of the International Monetary Fund. And of course, former world champion Garry Kasparov, who retired from chess for a (mostly unsuccessful) career in politics in Russia. However, the point is that women proportionally move more often to other careers than men.

REDUCING THE GENDER GAP

Although the presence of gender differences is undeniable in chess, the reasons behind them are poorly understood. Just like with STEM disciplines, biological and socio-cultural mechanisms are likely to be involved and to interact in complex ways. The explanation based on a glass ceiling effect is not as convincing as in other fields, partly because promotion in chess is based on highly objective measures – essentially, winning, drawing or losing a game. This being said, subtle factors might discourage girls and women to engage in chess. The least likely explanation seems to be that based on psychoanalysis.

There have been many initiatives, both personal and institutional, to improve women's skill level in chess. For example, some tournament organisers have tried to improve women's motivation by offering equal prizes for the two genders. There has been a trend to encourage mixed tournaments at the international level, by inviting more female players. At the local level, chess clubs have tried to create a more attractive atmosphere for women by getting rid of stereotypes. At the personal level, top female players such as Judit Polgár and Hou Yifan have systematically avoided female-only tournaments – sometimes even spurning the female world championship – in order to challenge leading male grandmasters and gain valuable experience.

6

STYLE AND INTUITION

In chess, style concerns the characteristics of one's knowledge and thinking that affect the kind of moves one chooses. One of the attractions of chess is that it is possible to play with widely different styles. There is no standard way of describing a player's style, but the following dimensions are often used: tactical (combinational) – strategic (positional); aggressive – defensive; risky – safe; and classic – original. Other classifications characterise styles as technical, dynamic and tricky. Style correlates with the number of moves that are normally anticipated: a tactical style requires deep calculations, whilst a strategic style calls for shallower calculations. Whatever their style, players need competency in most aspects of chess. For example, a player with a technical style but little tactical knowledge would be easy prey for any opponent that has identified his or her weakness in dealing with combinations.

THREE PROTOTYPICAL STYLES

Chess books tend to focus on three styles: psychological (where one plays the opponent rather than the position), positional and tactical. This section provides a description of these three styles with examples of top players who used them.

Emmanuel Lasker, world champion from 1894 to 1921, was one of the earliest and best proponents of the psychological style. He argued that, in order to win in chess, one had to understand one's opponents, his strengths and weaknesses, his likes and dislikes. The game is a fight between two personalities: "It is two human beings who fight on the chessboard, not the wooden pieces". Thus, one should play moves that are the most unpleasant for a specific opponent, rather than the objectively best moves. Garry Kasparov is a later world champion that excelled in the psychological style, as noted in Chapter 3, although he could also be categorised as a combinational player.

The positional style consists of playing sound moves that avoid creating weaknesses in one's position. Rather than starting a direct attack, which often leads to strategic concessions, positional players prefer to defend temporarily. One of the greatest proponents of this style was the Cuban José Raúl Capablanca, who was world champion from 1921 to 1927. Capablanca excelled in converting small positional or material advantages, playing with extreme precision – he was called the "chess machine" at the time. His style was highly economical, eschewing any superfluous complications. In spite of playing moves that looked harmless, Capablanca was a master in coordinating his pieces, exploiting their potentialities to their maximum. While not a tactical player per se, Capablanca was also able to calculate very precisely when necessary. World champions Anatoly Karpov and Magnus Carlsen are other highly skilled representatives of this style.

The combinational style focuses on direct attacks, drawing on tactical ideas to implement plans. One of the best examples of this style was Russo-French Alexander Alekhine, who held the world crown from 1927 to 1935 and from 1937 to 1946. Alekhine's play was very dynamic, trying to build direct attacks against the opponent. Of course, he also took sound positional principles into account, in particular making sure that his initiative was worth the strategic weaknesses that he conceded. Alekhine's genius was to display great imagination and risky play whilst at the same time remaining objective. Other world champions that adopted the combinational style are Mikhail Tal and Garry Kasparov.

In chess history, many players developed styles that were truly universal. If the position was calm and called for manoeuvring, they would play smooth positional play. If the position was dynamic and tactical, they would calculate deeply and accurately. If they were facing an endgame, they would display flawless technique. If the position called for psychological warfare, they would play the opponent. World champion Boris Spassky and grandmaster Fabiano Caruana, currently number 2 in the world and the youngest grandmaster from both the US and Italy, are examples of this universal style. With the advent of chess engines and chess databases, which have raised the overall level of play, increasingly more players have developed such a style, as being limited in some aspects of the game is just too risky from a competitive point of view.

DOES ONTOGENY RECAPITULATE PHYLOGENY?

Swiss psychologist Jean Piaget famously proposed in his theory of genetic epistemology that, with respect to knowledge, ontogeny parallels phylogeny. That is, during development children go through the same cognitive structures as their human ancestors during evolution. Interestingly, world champion Max Euwe proposed the same idea with chess. In his book *The Development of Chess Style*, he argued that the development of a chess player reflects the historical development of chess styles. Thus, players go through several stages, which can be mapped onto leading players of the time.

After an initial period where players moved their queen and other pieces rather erratically, hoping for a decisive opportunity (Gioachino Greco, 1600–1634), players realised the importance of pawns, their strengths and weaknesses (François André Danican Philidor, 1726–1795). Two combinational periods followed. First, combinations for their own sake, where beauty and attacking ideas dominated over material (Adolf Anderssen, 1818–1879). Then, combinations played for crowning deep positional play (Paul Morphy, 1837–1884). The next stage focused on strategy, and is the period when a sophisticated theory of positional play, now known as classical style, was almost single-handedly elaborated by Wilhelm Steinitz (1836–1900). Key principles include the occupation of the centre, the avoidance of pawn weaknesses and the accumulation of small advantages.

This was followed by a period where positional play got mastered to the point where it became pure technique (1900–1914; José Raúl Capablanca is the best example of this period). In reaction to this stage dominated by technique but also dogmatism and a lack of creativity, a number of grandmasters came up with revolutionary ideas, which essentially violated the key principles laid out by Steinitz. Key actors in this period (1919–1940) include Richard Réti, Alexander Alekhine and Aron Nimzowitsch. Euwe's final stage is called the Russian School, and starts in 1945. It is characterised by an emphasis on the initiative and dynamic piece play, fighting spirit, counter-play and active defence.

Euwe's thesis is intriguing but unfortunately not developed in great depth. It seems reasonable for the early stages of a player's career. Beginners do enjoy wandering with their queen, giving checks and grabbing material. And this is rapidly followed by a stage where they realise – thanks to their teacher, books, videos or painful defeats – that pawns matter and that their structure dictates much of the game. At this point, I believe that Euwe's thesis falls apart: styles diverge from rather than parallel chess history. Some players focus on dynamic and combinational play; others on positional and technical play; and still others try to have a more universal style. Nowadays, style is mostly determined by the kind of openings played, and it is not uncommon for a player to have a defensive positional style with Black and an aggressive combinational style with White. In addition, opening theory has developed to such a point that moves are determined more by knowledge than by style. Even within the same opening, and depending on the variation chosen by the opponent, a player will alternatively play positionally, tactically and technically. Finally, the good old times where mastering one style was enough to reach the international level are over: the overall level of chess has increased to such an extent that at least good knowledge and know-how of the main styles is essential for competing professionally.

A different approach to style might be mentioned here. Using psychoanalysis, Reuben Fine analysed the styles of world champions with respect to their personality. He concluded that the relationship is not straightforward. In some cases, players with an aggressive personality do attack on the chessboard (e.g. Alekhine). In other cases, it is the opposite: players who are aggressive in life defend in chess (e.g. Steinitz).

A COMPUTER STUDY OF STYLE IN CHESS

In a controversial paper written in 2006, Guid and Bratko used computer analyses to find out who was the best player ever. They used a slightly modified version of Crafty, a very strong computer programme, to assess the quality of the moves played in world championship matches, starting from the 1886 match between Zukertort and Steinitz. Fourteen world champions, from Steinitz to Kasparov, disputed these matches. Discarding the first 11 moves of each game, as they tend to rely on chess theory – which has improved over the years – Guid and Bratko calculated the difference in quality between the move proposed by the computer programme and the move actually played in the game.

The results showed that the players choosing the moves the closest to Crafty's were Capablanca, Kramnik and Karpov. These three players were also, with Petrosian, the players with the lowest blunder rate. By contrast, the three players who were the farthest from Crafty's choices – Botvinnik, Euwe and Steinitz – were also the three players with the highest blunder rate. With respect to style, Steinitz, Tal and Fischer had the highest position complexity on average, while Petrosian, Spassky and in particular Capablanca managed to keep their games at a fairly low level of complexity. Guid and Bratko concluded that the latter players, who can be described as calm and positional, tended to play simpler positions, and thus on average played better moves and avoided blunders. When a measure combining complexity and error was used, the most precise players turned out to be Kramnik, Capablanca and Karpov, in that order.

Whilst thought-provoking, this study has raised a number of criticisms from the chess community. One of them is that Crafty was not the best computer programme at the time, and indeed was weaker, based on the Elo rating, than some of the world champions investigated. Another is that, even with current computer programmes that are vastly superior both to the version of Crafty used in that study and the best human players, there is sometimes a fair amount of disagreement in the way they evaluate a move, in particular when the position is complex. This brings us to the third point: it is clear that Crafty did not "understand" some of the most brilliant human moves, which relied either on calculations deeper than what Crafty could perform or on subtle positional considerations. There also seems to be a bias in favour of positional players, who prefer calm positions in which it is difficult to commit a serious error. Fourth, the style of some players changed during their career; a notable example is Steinitz, who played wild tactical games in his youth before adopting a defensive style in the second part of his career. Finally, this analysis totally ignores psychological aspects. Given their style, players such as Lasker, Tal and Botvinnik were often playing more the opponent than the position itself, with obvious success but also with many errors from an objective point of view. In that respect, Siegbert Tarrasch might have had the last word: "One doesn't have to play well, it's enough to play better than your opponent".

WHAT IS INTUITION?

Intuition can be defined as the ability to understand a situation rapidly and effortlessly. It is a topic that has been of great interest both to psychologists and chess players. The former consider it as one of the defining features of expertise – think of a medical doctor able to diagnose a disease almost immediately. The latter wonder how a player like Magnus Carlsen is so good at finding good moves, often without much calculation, while weaker grandmasters cannot find them despite considerable thinking. Also, how is it that the same concept – intuition – is used to describe players with styles as opposite as world champion Tigran Petrosian (who excelled in calm, solid and strategic positions) and world champion Mikhail Tal (who relished wild combinational play crowned by risky sacrifices)?

According to psychologists, experts' intuition is characterised by several features: speed and ease of understanding the problem and finding a solution; perceptual and holistic nature of that understanding (i.e. the problem is understood as a whole); absence of awareness of how the solution is reached; and presence of emotions. A final requirement, to avoid the case where people just guess, is that intuitions must be correct most of the time. In most domains, experts display intuitions with routine problems. However, as problems get more complex and harder, experts tend to revert to problem-solving methods that are non-intuitive and rely on conscious problem-solving.

Chess has been the main topic of study behind many groundbreaking works on intuition. In his PhD thesis, de Groot emphasised the importance of intuition, and actually argued that it is part of most of our thinking, even with difficult problems, which at first sight seem to be addressed with conscious, analytical methods. In the 1960s, Oleg Tikhomirov stressed the link between intuition and emotions. It is perhaps surprising that this connection was first made by Tikhomirov, a psychologist who was Soviet, Marxist and materialist. Finally, as we have seen in chapters 1 and 2, Simon and Chase argue that intuition is pattern recognition, and provided a theory of how pattern recognition was made possible by the acquisition of a large number of chunks.

FIVE-STAGE THEORY OF INTUITION

Chess was also used extensively in *Mind over Matter: The Power of Human Intuition and Expertise in the Era of the Computer*, an influential book written by philosopher Hubert Dreyfus and mathematician Stuart Dreyfus. The Dreyfus brothers proposed that the road to expertise consists of five stages. In the *novice stage*, information about domain-related facts, features and actions is acquired through instruction. The application of this knowledge is fairly mechanical, and particularities of the environment are ignored. After considerable concrete experience, individuals move to the next stage, the *advanced beginner stage*. The context becomes increasingly significant and used for making decisions. In the *competence stage*, efficiency increases and decision-making methods are coordinated hierarchically. However, planning is essentially still conscious and intentional. Intuitive understanding makes its appearance in the *proficiency stage*, and individuals learn to pay attention to salient features and ignore others. However, decisions still depend on analytical thinking. It is only in the final *expertise stage* that decisions are intuitive. At this stage, according to Dreyfus and Dreyfus, experts do not make decisions, they just carry out the right action. Except for very difficult problems, behaviour is entirely fluid. Think of Neo in *The Matrix* knocking down an army of Smiths as if he was walking in the park, and you get the picture.

While the theory does describe important characteristics of the development of expertise (e.g. importance of context, progress from hesitant and error-prone to fluid behaviour and of course the role of intuition), it is seriously flawed, as I have shown in an article written with my PhD student Philippe Chassy. An important part of our analysis relies on chess. Dreyfus and Dreyfus argue that, at the expertise level, conscious problem-solving does not play any role. Even when grandmasters deliberate, for example when they face a difficult problem, they do not anticipate moves and carry out other types of analytical thinking, but rather they reflect on their intuitions. This is a very surprising statement. How about the substantial amount of research, starting with de Groot's work in the 1940s, supporting the presence of look-ahead search? A few years ago, I attended a workshop on expertise held in Hubert Dreyfus's honour, and asked him the question. He answered that he was not aware of this research. Rather disappointedly, one of the most cited works on expertise and intuition got it totally wrong with respect to the empirical evidence on chess thinking!

Dreyfus and Dreyfus did mention an interesting informal experiment. International master Julio Kaplan played rapid games against a weaker master whilst adding dictated numbers at the same time. In spite of the interfering task, Kaplan "more than held his own". This was taken as evidence that experts can still display fluid behaviour despite lacking time for planning. This is a reasonable conclusion, although it hard to evaluate the experiment given the few details provided. Unfortunately for the theory, when a proper experiment was carried out by Robbins and colleagues, where players had to generate random numbers while solving tactical chess problems, it was found that players were affected by the interfering task. With the group of stronger players, performance dropped by about one third when compared to the control condition where they simply solved chess problems.

COMPUTERS AND INTUITION

In a previous book written in 1972, *What Computers Can't Do*, Hubert Dreyfus had provided a blistering criticism of the then nascent field of artificial intelligence. His key argument was that, while computers can reach decent levels by analytical means (such as anticipating a large number of moves in chess), they would never be able to reach genuine expertise, because they lack intuition. Developments in artificial intelligence have proven Dreyfus wrong. Checkers world champion Marion Tinsley was beaten by Chinook in 1994. A similar fate has met world champions in other board games: in chess, Garry Kasparov was beaten by Deep Blue in 1997; in Othello, Takeshi Murakami was beaten by Logistello in 1997; finally, in Go, which was considered out of reach of artificial intelligence, Lee Sedol was beaten by AlphaGo in 2016. In all these domains, computers are now vastly superior to humans. For example, in chess, the current number one player in the world Magnus Carlsen has an Elo rating of 2843 whilst the best computer programme, Stockfish 9, has a rating of 3450. With a difference of about 600 points, or 3 standard deviations, Carlsen is expected to score only 3 points out of 100 games.

Computer intuition

Progress in artificial intelligence has two important implications for our understanding of human intuition. First, it raises the possibility that computers not only play chess better than humans, but that they understand it more deeply and have a much better intuition. This is a repulsive thought for most human players, but it is probably a reality now. Most computer programmes playing chess are based on powerful evaluation functions, combining dozens of features, such as safety of the king, mobility of the White-square bishop and control of centre, with the ability of searching billions of positions before selecting a move. Still, it is totally out of the question to calculate all possibilities, and thus computers rely on some form of "intuition" to make a move. In fact, there are many examples of surprising moves played by computers, which turned out after extensive human analyses to be very deep positionally. In 2006, world champion Vladimir Kramnik lost 4–2 against Deep Fritz, which actually was not even the best computer programme at the time. In the 6th game, Deep Fritz played a rook manoeuvre that pundits derided as child-like. The next moves of the game showed that this manoeuvre was the prelude to a very deep plan that led to fatal weaknesses in Kramnik's king's side and ultimately to material loss.

If there were any doubts that artificial intuition is possible, these were recently shattered by AlphaGo's victories in Go. Just before the entrance of AlphaGo into the Go scene in 2015, artificial intelligence had progressed very slowly with this game, to the point that some experts thought that computers would never be able to beat the best humans. The most optimistic researchers were of the view that it would take a computer at least 10 years to win a game against a Go professional player. Thus, before the match against South Korean grandmaster Lee Sedol, spirits were high in the Go community and it was expected that AlphaGo would be beaten easily. After all, Lee Sedol was only one of two players to have won 18 international titles (more or less the equivalent to Grand Slam titles in tennis). Unfortunately for humankind, Lee was thrashed 4–1.

AlphaGo primarily used three artificial intelligence techniques: deep learning, reinforcement learning and Monte Carlo tree search. Deep learning consists of sophisticated methods for adjusting the weights of an artificial neural network, using grandmaster games as input. Reinforcement learning further adjusts these weights, taking into account the result of a game following a given move. Monte Carlo tree search, in a nutshell, generates games by randomly picking moves for the two players. This is quite different from the technique traditionally used in computer chess (e.g. Deep Blue or Deep Fritz), where possible moves are explored in a systematic way. The rationale is that, when averaging a large number of games, better moves in the current position lead to better results even with random games.

AlphaGo was undoubtedly a milestone in artificial intelligence research, but that was only the beginning. An improved version beat Chinese grandmaster Ke Jie, the world's No. 1, with a 3–0 score, and won all sixty online games it played against world-class players. About AlphaGo's strength, Ke Jie said the following: "After humanity spent thousands of years improving our tactics, computers tell us that humans are completely wrong. . . . I would go as far as to say not a single human has touched the edge of the truth of Go". As if this was not enough, a new version of the programme, called AlphaZero, learns from scratch and improves by playing against itself. That is, except for the rules of the game, it creates all its knowledge. Alpha-Zero is superior to the previous versions; for example, it won 100–0 against the version that beat Lee Sedol. The rating of this version is a stunning 5000 Elo, compared to the 3700 Elo obtained by the best human Go player. (Note that ratings in Go are not directly comparable to ratings in chess.)

In an unpublished paper, the DeepMind team claimed that a generalised version of AlphaZero beat Stockfish, one of the best computer programmes in chess, and Elmo, the leading programme of shogi (Japanese chess), needing only 24 hours of learning to achieve a "superhuman level of play". The chess community has reacted strongly to this news, arguing that the match against Stockfish was unfair. For example, AlphaZero ran on dedicated hardware, and thus had much more processing power than Stockfish and Elmo, which ran on PCs. In addition, each programme had one minute to make a move, whilst Stockfish has been designed to optimise its time use, playing rapidly for obvious moves and thus saving time for more complex moves. These criticisms might be true, but the fact is that we have now a super-program that learns by itself from scratch and that plays much better than the best humans. In addition, AlphaZero has a very intriguing and intuitive style, sacrificing material for long-term positional compensations that most humans cannot see. Just like Go, AlphaZero seems to show that human understanding of chess, in spite of centuries of practice and study, is rather limited.

Lessons for human intuition

Progress in computer science and artificial intelligence gives scientists powerful tools for studying intuition and indeed rationality. An earlier try in this direction was carried out by Peter Jansen in 1992. He took advantage of the presence of chess endgame databases that have perfect knowledge of the value of each move and thus know what is the outcome of a position with perfect play on both sides. (At the time of writing, such databases have been built for all endgames with up to seven pieces.) Jansen found that even the best humans played poorly – as compared to optimal play – in simple endgames. For example, winning the endgame king-queen versus king-rook is considered trivial and is hardly discussed in textbooks. Jansen's results showed that world-class grandmasters committed so many mistakes that they needed, on average, four times longer than necessary to win the game. Because of the 50-move rule – which states that a game is a draw if 50 consecutive moves for White and Black are played without the capture of a piece or the movement of a pawn – they would have in many cases failed to win the game against the best defence.

7

ERRARE HUMANUM EST

To err is human. This certainly applies to chess players. Errors, including horrible howlers, are fairly common in chess. Most players, including world champions, blunder every so often, and the technical literature on chess provides some spectacular examples. In the game Petrosian against Bronstein in 1956, played in the Amsterdam qualification tournament for the world championship, future world champion Petrosian was winning but did not see that his queen was attacked. When Bronstein took her, Petrosian resigned on the spot. In the game Alekhine against Euwe, played in the world championship return match in 1937, both players overlooked a simple combination for three moves in a row. More recently, during the 2017 Wijk aan Zee tournament, world champion Magnus Carlsen missed a checkmate in three moves in his game against Anish Giri and let his lucky opponent escape with a draw. Worst of all, in his match against computer programme Deep Fritz, world champion Vladimir Kramnik overlooked a mate-in-one and was painfully checkmated.

Relatively little scientific research has been carried out on errors in chess. De Groot's thesis has some mentions in passing and a few studies have used blunders, typically identified by chess computers, as a dependent variable. The only detailed qualitative analysis trying to understand the mechanisms leading to errors was carried out by

Pertti Saariluoma. He induced errors by choosing combinations that could be found only by identifying two themes in close succession. As expected, most of the errors were made with the move that linked the two themes. Similar results were obtained with strategic positions and endgames. Saariluoma concluded by arguing that working memory overload explains errors only in part, and that it is necessary to develop more sophisticated explanations based on pattern recognition, planning and problem restructuring. This study explored an unchartered topic and called for more experiments; for example, one could try to induce specific errors as a way of testing different theories of chess skill.

By contrast, there are numerous discussions of errors in chess, and how to avoid them, in the practical chess literature. Alexander Kotov's *Think like a Grandmaster* and Nikolai Krogius's *Psychology in Chess*, which both present instructive and thought-provoking examples from grandmaster play, are good examples of such books. While their discussions are based on observations, anecdotes and a fair amount of speculation – explanations are often based on introspection, hindsight and a posteriori accounts – the described errors are real.

Kotov and Krogius provide several explanations for errors in chess. Some of the explanations are specific to chess, whilst others apply to other endeavours as well. Let us start with the domain specific ones.

AUTOMATISMS

Automatisms are important in chess, since they allow one to make decisions rapidly. Some consist of very simple conditioned actions, such as "if your opponent takes one of your pieces, take it back immediately", or "if a piece is attacked, move it away". Others are subtler and directly link to the chunking mechanisms discussed in chapters 2 and 3. For example, given a certain pawn structure, it is often a good idea to place one's knight in front of an isolated pawn. The beauty of chess is that it is a game of exceptions, and even the best procedural knowledge will be incorrect every so often. If one follows one's intuition without doubling-checking variations concretely, there is always a risk that some tactical blow will be overlooked.

CHESS IMAGES

Krogius spends a great deal of time with what he calls "chess images". The term is maybe not the best one, as these images contain not only visual information on the location of pieces, but also more conceptual information such as the evaluation of the position. In some of Krogius's examples, images really refer to what I have called schemas or templates in previous chapters. Chess images are very useful in most cases, as they provide much information. They can also produce powerful negative effects, however. For example, facing an unexpected move by the opponent, a player will often still think using the mind-set provided by a chess image that was suitable just one move ago, and might miss a new opportunity. Several examples will be provided below.

Another class of errors, which Krogius calls "retained images", concerns the case where, when anticipating a sequence of moves, a piece taken by the opponent somehow still remains present in the mind's eye. The difficulty thus resides in correctly updating the location of pieces or their disappearance in the mind's eye. For example, with this type of error, a player would defend in his calculation against a bishop that actually is not on the board anymore. In a related type of errors, which Krogius calls "inert images", the player automatically carries a positive evaluation reached at some point of the game on to the following moves and is essentially on an automatic pilot mode. As a consequence, the difficulty of winning the game can be underestimated and one's sense of danger blunted. So, for example in the game Petrosian against Korchnoi in the 1963 Moscow tournament, Petrosian had had a winning position since the opening. Still winning after 34 moves, he overlooked a simple combination and played a careless move, which lost immediately. This type of error is related to overconfidence, which I shall discuss towards the end of this chapter. It is also related to the Einstellung effect that I described in Chapter 3. In this respect, Krogius reports a very interesting comment by Petrosian: "Personally, I am convinced that if a strong master does not see such a threat at once he will not notice it, even if he analyses the position for twenty to thirty minutes".

Many errors are due to attention lapses. A typical example is the case where one player misses an obvious threat, such as in the example above where Petrosian lost his queen in one move. To some extent, it could be argued that at least some of the errors that Krogius imputed to chess images are in fact attentional errors. In some cases, it seems that the effort required for anticipating moves wipes out from working memory important information, such as an attack against one's queen.

EMOTIONAL FACTORS

It might come as a surprise for non-players, but chess can be a very emotional game. To begin with, most players have their *bêtes noires*, opponents against whom their score is much less than expected by their relative objective strength. For example, Soviet grandmaster Efim Geller was the bête noire of Bobby Fischer, with five wins, three defeats and two draws, in spite of Fischer's superiority. Similarly, American grandmaster Hikaru Nakamura, currently number 8 in the world, struggles against Magnus Carlsen, having lost 12 games and won only one, with 21 draws. Krogius reports that he analysed 80 games between 10 pairs of players where one player was a bête noire for the other. He found that the players on the losing side committed more obvious strategic errors and tactical mistakes against their bête noire than against other players. Krogius argues that a negative emotional state strongly diminishes these players' vigilance and nervous resistance, although it could be argued that, in addition to this, there might be a profound incompatibility in style. For example, in the case of Fischer and Geller, Geller was known for his very dangerous, uncompromising attacking style. Interestingly, bêtes noires are not transitive. For example, ignoring draws, Tal had a lifetime score of 8–5 against Bronstein, and Bronstein had a lifetime score of 7–4 against Keres. However, rather than Tal dominating Keres, as predicted by a transitive relation, it is Keres who led by 8–4!

The opponent's behaviour is another important emotional factor that might cause distraction and irritation. The noise he is making when drinking his coffee, the way he is looking at you, his after-shave . . . pretty much anything might exasperate you. In the 1959 candidates' tournament, Hungarian grandmaster Pal Benko accused future world champion Mikhail Tal of hypnotising him, and decided to wear dark eyeglasses when playing against him. (This is another example of a bête noire, as Benko had lost the last five previous games against Tal.) The game ended in a draw, which is all what Tal needed to qualify for the world championship match against Botvinnik. After the game, Tal quipped: "When I want to win against Benko I win; when I want to draw, I draw!"

Emotional hatred and accusations of hypnosis were taken to new heights in the 1978 world championship match in Baguio between Viktor Korchnoi and Anatoly Karpov. Karpov included in his team Vladimir Zukhar, who at the time was a renowned parapsycholo-gist and hypnotist in Soviet Union. Korchnoi complained and started wearing reflecting glasses. (This is only one of the many bizarre incidents that single out this world championship.) Whether or not hypnosis really played a role, I doubt it. But it is true that Korchnoi – although admittedly playing some brilliant chess at times – made terrible mistakes in some games. For example, in the 17th game, he committed a string of errors which turned a winning position into a drawn position, in which he blundered and overlooked a simple checkmate in three moves.

A final source of emotional pressure is one's position in the tour-nament and the possibility of achieving an important result. In 1988, I was playing the tournament of my life in Biel and was very close to obtaining a grandmaster norm, a key requirement for becom-ing a grandmaster. I would have been the first Swiss player to do so. My opponent was former women's world champion Nona Gap-rindashvili. After some energetic and precise play in the opening and early middle game, I obtained a winning position against her unconventional defensive system. However, at the crucial moment, I missed a simple move that meant winning straight away, progressively lost the thread and ultimately had to resign. There is no doubt in my mind that my defeat was due to the fact that I could not handle the pressure of being so close to a grandmaster norm. How to regulate emotions is of course an important topic in other sports as well, and is indeed a standard topic in sports psychology.

INSUFFICIENT KNOWLEDGE

Many errors are caused by a lack of knowledge. At weaker levels, this can be due to not knowing typical openings, standard tactical and strategic patterns in the middle game and common manoeuvres in endgames. As noted in an earlier chapter, masters and grandmasters often win games by waiting for mistakes, and lack of knowledge is at the core of many of them. Mistakes due to insufficient knowledge also occasionally occur at the top level. For example, in the first game of the world championship held in 2010 in Sofia between Veselin Topalov and Viswanathan Anand, world champion Anand could not remember the move order of a variation he had prepared in depth. He chose the wrong order and got thrashed by his opponent, who had remembered the brilliant combination that refuted Anand's move.

TIME TROUBLE

Competitive games are played with a clock, and thinking time is limited. The limit is strict and overstepping one's thinking time means defeat by "losing on time", which is not uncommon. An extreme case is grandmaster Friedrich Sämisch, one of the leading players in the 1920s, who lost every single game on time in two tournaments in 1969, when he was 73 years old. The exact time limits vary from tournament to tournament, but there has been a tendency towards a decrease of thinking time over the years, partly to reduce the duration of games and make them more exciting. Currently, many tournaments use time controls of 90 minutes for the first 40 moves, followed by

30 minutes to finish the game, with each player receiving an increment of 30 seconds after each move.

Before the 1990s, it was common for each player to have 2 hours 30 minutes for 40 moves, and then 1 hour for each sequence of 20 moves. Games used to be interrupted ("adjourned") after 5 hours of play, and resumed later in the day or the next day. This break was meant to allow players to rest and eat. In practice, it also allowed players and their seconds to analyse the current position. There used to be an interesting literature describing the excitements and pitfalls of analysing adjourned games, and about how to do it properly. However, with the advent of powerful computers, which pretty much find the optimal sequence of moves for both sides, it became clear that adjournments were becoming meaningless as the human factor simply disappeared. The practice of adjourning games progressively died out in the mid-1990s, with the added advantage that games are now played in one go, which is much more enthralling from the spectators' point of view.

Whatever the exact time controls, it is common for some players to think for long periods in the opening and at the beginning of the middle game, when they face critical decisions. As a consequence, they have little thinking left at the end, and are in *time trouble*, or in *zeitnot*, a German word commonly used by chess players. The exact definition varies from player to player. For some, having less than 1 minute per move is considered as time trouble; for others, having to play 10 moves in 5 minutes is nothing special. Players vary considerably as to whether they are likely to be in time trouble. Some players are in zeitnot in nearly every game, and are used to playing 20 moves in 2 or 3 minutes. Others systematically avoid any time shortage.

During time trouble, short-term tactics dominate over long-term strategies, intuition comes before look-ahead search and concrete ideas take precedence over abstract considerations. Simple heuristics are used, such as "simplify positions by trading pieces off", "restore material balance rather than play for the initiative" and "if possible, postpone making important decisions until the end of the zeitnot". Because decisions have to be made rapidly and calculations are superficial, blunders occur often. In general, the advice is to not be in time trouble. As world champion Alekhine wrote in criticising one of his moves: "A horrible move, and in my opinion the fact that White was in time trouble when he made it is no more justification than the claim of a law breaker that he was drunk when he committed the crime".

Alekhine's comment might be too one-sided. There is actually an interesting trade-off with respect to decision-making. Not spending enough time on critical moments in the game might lead to playing inferior moves, losing the advantage in a superior position or not defending a difficult position properly. Thus, being in zeitnot might be a worthwhile price to pay. On the other hand, many players simply cannot make up their minds, sometimes because they want to find the optimal move rather than to play a move that is good enough. An interesting question, which to my knowledge has not been studied, is whether there is a link between being addicted to time trouble in chess and procrastination in life outside chess.

Many tragedies have happened in zeitnot, with winning positions being destroyed in one move. My game against grandmaster Lubomir Ftacnik in the 1984 Biel tournament is a good example of this. After a complicated game where my opponent progressively outplayed me, we were in a mutual time trouble. My opponent made a terrible mistake five moves before the time limit, overlooking a simple checkmate in two moves. His blunder is also a good example of an error caused by a conditioned reflex. He thought that attacking my rook with a pawn would force my rook to move away, while in fact moving my queen created an unstoppable checkmate threat.

This example illustrates the case where being in zeitnot is a rational decision. My position had vastly deteriorated in the last 10 moves, and was clearly lost. Thus, the only practical chance was to create a situation – a reciprocal time trouble – where the logic of chess could be perturbed by random factors and by putting psychological pressure on the opponent. While the choice to be in time trouble was rational from my point of view, it was a mistake from the point of view of my opponent. I hasten to add that such an analysis is easy with hindsight, but much harder to make during the excitement of the game. In fact, I found myself in Ftacnik's unhappy situation in several of my own games, losing a winning game because of blunders caused by lack of time.

How to behave when one is in time trouble? Should one try to exploit or not the opponent's time trouble? These are important practical questions, and much ink has been spilled on them. Krogius answers the first question by advising to keep one's concentration and avoiding distracting thoughts. If one has a plan, one should follow it; else, the best option is to use waiting tactics, since there is simply not enough time to come up with a sound plan. He also recommends trying to find the goal of each opponent's move, even by consciously asking questions such as "What is the threat?" Finally, he advocates using auto-suggestion techniques such as verbal commands, the efficacy of which has been documented in sports. As for Kotov, his main advice is simply to avoid getting into zeitnot. If this not possible, the main thing is to remain calm and to play as if one were not in time trouble. Basically, to do the same as normal, just quicker. According to him, this is what top players are doing.

There is some disagreement about how to handle an opponent's zeitnot. On the one hand, both Krogius and Kotov agree on a few points. One should control one's nerves, stay calm and evaluate the position objectively. In particular, one should not get excited or irritated by the opponent's behaviour. Note that this is not always easy, as players with few seconds on their clock are sometimes in a state of extreme agitation if not outright panic. Both also advise against complicating the position for the sake of it, and against speeding up one's play to prevent the opponent from thinking during one's own time, as this is likely to lead to errors. Where they disagree is whether anything at all should be done to capitalise on the opponent's shortage of time. Krogius recommends calculating a sequence of four or five moves, which if possible change the nature of the position (e.g. moving from a middle game to an endgame), and to play them quickly, in the hope to take one's opponent unaware. Kotov disagrees, and points out that this is likely to lead to mistakes on the part of the player who has sufficient time. Rather, he endorses world champion Vasily Smyslov's advice of leaving the board and coming back only after the opponent has played a move. Thus, Kotov's general recommendation is to fully ignore one's opponent's time trouble.

TIREDNESS, OVERCONFIDENCE AND HABITUATION

This section briefly discusses a few additional sources of errors. An obvious one is tiredness; after a long and difficult game, or after several days or weeks of playing in a tournament, one is bound to become tired. International master Charles Partos, who coached Biel in the Swiss team championship, used to bring bananas and chocolate after 4 hours of play to replenish players' glucose stores and thus provide energy for the brain – a sound application of nutritional principles. The long-term advice to avoid tiredness is to be fit physically, and many world champions such as Boris Spassky, Bobby Fischer, Garry Kasparov and Magnus Carlsen practiced several sports and were in top physical condition when they won the title.

Another standard source of error, not only in chess but in other sports as well, is overconfidence. With overconfidence, vigilance goes down, attention becomes relaxed and possible dangers are ignored. The chess literature contains many examples, even at the top level, where the proximity of victory led to overconfidence, a decrease in the quality of play and often errors that turn a win into a draw or, worse, a loss. Related to overconfidence is the desire to win a game by a flashy combination rather than by prosaic methods. As objectivity gets lost, the "brilliant" combination often turns out to be flawed and the opponent escapes with a lucky draw or even a win.

I have once been victim of an interesting kind of mistake, which I have not found reported in the chess literature, and which might be related to the mechanism of *habituation*. In animal psychology, habituation is a kind of learning where a response to a stimulus decreases or even stops after repeated exposure. In my game against former world champion Boris Spassky at the Reggio Emilia tournament in 1983,

I chose a very sharp variation and had the advantage after the opening. For several moves, I considered a pawn sacrifice in the centre in order to initiate a direct attack against Spassky's king. However, the idea never worked satisfactorily, so I progressively directed my attention to another central break. Ironically, at the very moment where I gave up on my initial idea, it would have in fact been the winning move.

HOW TO AVOID ERRORS?

Chess coaches have provided many recommendations for avoiding errors. Some of them are rather obvious and simply aim to eliminate the source of the errors I have discussed. For example, one should be aware of automatisms, control one's emotions, make sure that one's knowledge is up-to-date, relax and get enough sleep before an important game and avoid time trouble. Some more general recommendations have also been made, which tend to take action against mind-set effects. A piece of good advice is to look at one's position from the point of view of the opponent. This is meant literally: one should every so often physically stand behind one's opponent and have a look at the position. This is actually not bad advice – maybe in a more figurative way – for many other avenues of life where one is likely to hold preconceptions.

Kotov encourages players to use Blumenfeld's rule, named after Soviet master Benjamin Blumenfeld, who was also a psychologist. The idea is to make sure that one does not miss the obvious, even after having spent dozens of minutes analysing a position. After having selected a move, one should write it down on one's score sheet, *before actually playing it*. (In tournaments, players are required to write down their moves and their opponents', as an official record of the game. This can be useful, for example, to ascertain whether the required number of moves have been played before the time control.) Kotov emphasises that care should be taken to write the move neatly and clearly. He argues that, by doing so, one goes from the future possibilities of the game back to the here and now. A variant of this advice is to stop looking at the board and stare at some distant object in the room. Then, one should look again at the board, with fresh eyes, so to speak. This should make it possible to look at the position as it is on the board right now. The advice is now to stare at the position for about a minute, through the eyes of a novice, and ask very basic questions such as: is my queen attacked? Is there a direct threat against my king? According to Kotov, this double-checking procedure drastically decreases the risk of committing a blunder.

This is very good advice. Having used it in my chess career, I can vouchsafe that it saved me from an embarrassing oversight more than once. Unfortunately, one important part of Blumenfeld's rule is not possible anymore. The International Chess Federation has changed its rules, and moves must be written down on the score sheet *only after* they have been executed on the board.

8

PSYCHOLOGICAL WARFARE
AND TRAINING TECHNIQUES

There is a long-standing discussion in the literature as to whether chess is a sport, a science or an art. Curiously, the obvious fact that it is a game is rarely mentioned. World champion Emanuel Lasker argued that it is none of those. Rather, chess is a fight.

Lasker was certainly correct. In fact, this fight can be carried out with different means: from pure skill (e.g. an attack against a weak pawn), to subtle psychology (e.g. choosing an opening in which the opponent feels uncomfortable), to not-so-subtle psychology (e.g. trying to disturb one's opponent) and finally to outright cheating (e.g. using a computer). Skill is of course the province of the technical chess literature and is beyond the scope of this book. In the second part of this chapter, I shall limit myself to discussing ways to improve skill through training. But the other forms of fight are worth some discussion.

PLAYING THE OPPONENT

As noted by Lasker, chess is a battle between two personalities. Thus, it is sometimes advantageous to play the opponent rather than objectively strong moves. A tactical trap might be tried against a strategist, or wild complications might be introduced against a player preferring clear positions. Playing the opponent is increasingly required to score full points as players' technical level is getting extremely high, and simply playing the position might not be enough to win a game between two players of the same strength.

There is undoubtedly an element of risk in doing so. As Lasker clearly stated it, playing chess is, to some extent, an application of probability theory: knowing one's opponent's personality, tastes and dislikes makes it possible to estimate the probability that she would select a given move. It could be argued that all world champions and most top players excel in playing the opponent. In Chapter 3, I gave the example of Kasparov adopting a different style against each of his opponents in his simultaneous exhibition against the Swiss national team. Chess history provides some spectacular examples of this style of play.

Let us start with Lasker, the ultimate master of applied chess psychology. In order to win the St. Petersburg tournament in 1914, Lasker had to beat Capablanca with White. Everybody expected that Lasker would choose an aggressive or at least a complex opening. To general surprise, Lasker chose the exchange variation of the Spanish defence, which had the reputation of being a tame and drawish opening. To boot, he exchanged the queens after five moves, as if he had no intention of winning. Of course, Lasker knew what he was doing. The position required Capablanca to play actively to keep the balance, which he found difficult as he was aiming for a draw. Indeed, Capablanca played passively, and little by little Lasker was able to increase the mobility of his pieces and build a promising position. In a difficult situation, Capablanca overlooked an elegant combination, and had to resign a few moves after.

Another classic example is the overall strategy adopted by Alekhine in his 1927 match against Capablanca. After extensive analysis of Capablanca's games, Alekhine came to the conclusion that the Cuban, whilst a brilliant strategist, was weaker tactically. As consequence, he decided to systematically double-check Capablanca's plans for tactical errors, which did occur in the match. Being prepared, Alekhine was able to take advantage of them. The Franco-Russian grandmaster made another brilliant psychological move in this match. With Black, he used the defensive approach preferred by Capablanca, which was to simplify positions by trading pieces off and then rely on his technique to defend them. This approach was new to Alekhine, who in the past had used more risky and active methods of defence. However, the psychological surprise turned out to be more important than Alekhine's relative inexperience with this type of position.

THEORETICAL NOVELTIES

Knowing the "theory of openings" is essential for chess players. It is not a "theory" in the scientific meaning of the term – a set of mechanisms explaining a body of empirical phenomena. It is not even a set of principles. Rather, it is the compilation of moves that have been played in the past and their evaluation: did White or Black have the advantage, or was the position equal? This body of knowledge has grown rapidly in the last decades, and it is not uncommon for players to blitz 20 moves or more in the opening, playing them from memory. In a paper with Philippe Chassy, we estimated that masters must have memorised about 100,000 opening moves.

Then comes the much-anticipated moment where the game diverges from theory: a theoretical novelty. At the amateur level, novelties often reflect players' lack of knowledge. By contrast, at the professional level, many theoretical novelties are the fruit of home preparation, sometimes weeks or months before the actual game. In the quietness of their living room, players can spend hours and hours studying a position, moving the pieces on the board and even asking the advice of their colleagues. In the last two decades, players have increasingly used computers to help their investigations, which has multiplied the number of positions that can be studied by several orders of magnitude. As all this is done before the start of the game itself, it is legal. The aim of these analyses is not only to find the move that is objectively the best, but also to find moves that will confront the opponent with the kinds of positions they do not like or that are unknown to them. This can occasionally include inferior positions, especially with Black, with the idea that the opponent will not be able to find the winning plan in the limited time allowed by competitive games.

The 2008 world championship between Anand and Kramnik offered several impressive examples of this kind of preparation. For instance, in the third game, Anand, playing Black, selected a rare but very sharp defensive system. In the 17th move, he introduced a new move that sacrificed two pawns for a strong initiative. The line was highly tactical and risky, but also created the kind of position that was unpleasant for Kramnik. Indeed, the Russian grandmaster lost his way in the jungle of complications, and was not able to defend his position successfully.

INCREASING THE PSYCHOLOGICAL PRESSURE

Moving away from the chessboard, a number of techniques can be used to get on the opponent's nerves and disturb him. Whilst most players behave impeccably, these reprehensible techniques are used every so often. The options are endless: staring at the opponent intensively (photographs of chess players can be pretty boring, but some show pretty nasty looks!); arriving late for the game (used sometimes by Bobby Fischer); distracting the opponent by making noise stirring up one's coffee; smoking a strong cigar (one of Lasker's favourites); kicking the opponent with one's feet (occasionally done by Petrosian); or wearing a malodorous perfume. Thankfully, the rules of the International Chess Federation have evolved to avoid some of these tricks; smoking is now forbidden in the playing hall, and late arrivals are not always tolerated.

The idea of psychological pressure has sometimes been taken to surprising extremes. Fine reports that Joseph Henry Blackburne, a leading player in the second half of the 19th century, threw Steinitz out of the window after an argument. During the 1984 French championship, Gilles Andruet kept distracting Bachar Kouatly with all sorts of noises, even opening a beer loudly.

Kouatly: "Now, you stop, or I punch your face".
Andruet: "Go on, I dare you!"
Punch.

OUTRIGHT CHEATING

The last category consists of methods that clearly constitute cheating. Bobby Fischer accused Soviet grandmasters of such practices: according to him, they were rapidly drawing amongst themselves to conserve energy, were consulting during games and were even fixing games amongst themselves in tournaments. A 2006 study by Moul and Nye supports Fischer's view. Using statistical analyses, they showed that the rate of draws amongst Soviet grandmasters was higher in important international tournaments than in national tournaments.

Collusion is not uncommon nowadays. The classic example is the last round of a tournament, where a win would lead to prize money for one of two players facing each other, but a draw would not. The temptation is great for the two players to come to an agreement before the game, with, for example, the player losing the game getting more money than the winner. On a slightly more bizarre note, a number of tournaments were simply invented, for example in Rumania and Ukraine, with no games actually played, so that some players could win Elo points or be awarded the title of international master or even grandmaster.

Technology has created new opportunities for cheaters. Several players have been caught, during a competitive game, using a chess programme on their smartphone during breaks in the bathroom. One player, called the "James Bond of chess", hid a transmitter in his shoe in order to receive move suggestions sent by a friend. In the 2010 Olympiads, three French players used a sophisticated scheme for communicating moves. The first player took advantage of live Internet broadcasting of the tournament to follow the game from his home and analyse the current position with a computer programme. He would then text the best move to the second player, who would communicate it to the player actually playing the game, using his standing or sitting at various places as a code. The scheme was subtle, but had a not-so-subtle flaw: they used a mobile phone of the French Federation, which handed down heavy suspensions to the three players. To make such technological cheating harder, the International

Chess Federation has banned the use of mobile phones and other electronic devices in playing venues. In the same spirit, tournament organisers now increasingly add a lag to the transmission of moves on the Internet.

HOW TO PROGRESS – FROM BEGINNER TO CANDIDATE MASTER

Once beginners have learnt the basics of the games, which can easily be done using any one of the many introductory books or material on the Internet, the question arises: how to progress? This section deals with training methods suitable up to candidate master level. The following section deals with the kind of training that more ambitious players should adopt.

As mentioned in Chapter 4, a number of training methods are available to dedicated players. First, the basic tactical ideas should be learnt and mastered. Tactics are essential, as without the ability to see simple combinations it is impossible to implement any plan successfully. In addition, tactics sometimes can help change the course of a game that was strategically misplayed. Books on tactics typically consist of descriptions of standard motifs and then numerous exercises where one has to find the winning sequence of moves. This is the part of training that is the closest to deliberate practice. Second, one should assimilate the foundations of strategy and planning. A huge number of books and videos are available for teaching this material. The old classics by Euwe, Tarrasch and Nimzowitsch are still very useful, as they present the key ideas in a straightforward way. Of interest are also books focusing on defensive methods or on attacking methods. Third, endgames should be studied. This is where players develop their technique: methods for converting a material or strategic advantage into a win and methods for successfully defending inferior positions. The great classics by Fine, Averbakh and Dvoretsky are still good introductions.

Fourth, a fair amount of attention should be devoted to openings. It is useful to have basic knowledge of most openings, but players should specialise in particular openings and studying thoroughly. Here, the advice of a coach is particularly useful, since the amateur will be bewildered by the huge number of possible openings and variations. Importantly, studying openings does not solely mean learning the first moves of the game, but also assimilating typical strategic ideas and tactical themes. Thus, opening books will spend a fair amount of time discussing typical middle game positions or even endgames that often stem from a given opening.

The importance of opening specialisation might appear surprising, but it is in fact supported by empirical data. In a 2009 study, Merim Bilalić and colleagues asked players to find the best move in a given position. The players, who ranged from candidate masters to grandmasters, specialised either in the Winawer variation of the French defence or in the Najdorf variation of the Sicilian defence. The problems came from these two defences and from neutral positions, which were not typical of any specific opening. With positions outside the opening in which they specialised, players' performance was about 200 Elo points below their performance with familiar positions. The loss of performance is about one standard deviation in skill, which is enormous. For example, when facing a position outside their usual openings, a typical grandmaster (about 2600 Elo points) would perform at the level of an international master (about 2400 Elo points).

Thus, while part of chess knowledge is general and not related to any opening, opening-specific patterns and methods are also clearly important since some level of skill is lost when those cannot be used. Normally, the advice is to play the openings that one knows well, especially against stronger players. For a professional player, the night-mare scenario is to play an obscure tactical opening of which he has only a hazy memory against a much weaker amateur who obviously knows all its secrets.

Fifth, one should study the classics: famous historical games and games played by leading grandmasters, including, of course, world champions. This will provide a huge source of tactical and strategic ideas, as well as good examples of how to convert advantages into a win. Sixth, playing competitive games is an essential part of becoming a better player. Finally, it is important to analyse one's own games critically, if possible with a coach: What went wrong? What were the strengths of one's play? What could be improved?

This literature is essentially applied, in the sense that it is a compilation of principles and methods that have led to successful results. It is almost never based on scientific research. One of the rare exceptions, a paper I wrote with Peter Jansen, used template theory (see Chapter 2) to develop teaching principles. Our approach was guided by some of the central findings I have discussed in earlier chapters of this book. These include the limited capacity of attention and short-term memory, perceptual chunks, selective search and the fact that knowledge is domain specific. The approach also included more general principles of learning and memory, such as the importance of processing information deeply and ideally from different points of view.

Three educational principles were highlighted in the paper: the acquisition of knowledge should proceed from simple to complex; learning is more efficient when the teacher (or a book) clearly identifies the elements to be learnt; and finally, a powerful way of assisting learning is first to present the material in a simple, even over-simplified way, and then to return to it several times, each time adding new information. We called this method an *improving spiral*. For example, when studying an opening, a first pass would cover the main ideas of the opening and commonly played variations. A second pass would discuss some typical endgames frequent with this opening. The next pass could address strategic themes suggested by this opening's pawn structure. Not only will the student learn important information, but the multiple passes will also strengthen memory traces and combat the risk of forgetting. A variant of this is the *decomposition method*, where a typical opening position is studied by removing all pieces except kings and pawns, and the resulting endgame analysed or played in practice games. Different pieces are progressively added, and again the resulting endgames studied.

As is clear from my discussion of chess knowledge in Chapter 2, chess expertise consists in great part of mastering common methods of play. Thus, while time should be devoted to find-the-best-move exercises, practice games and analysis, the main ideas should be explicitly taught and open-ended forms of teaching such as that advocated by the discovery-based learning approach should be avoided. After all, it took several centuries for very smart people to discover these ideas!

HOW TO PROGRESS – FROM CANDIDATE MASTER TO GRANDMASTER

In a sense, training for reaching higher levels is more of the same: a hearty regime of opening theory, tactics, strategy and endgames. The literature becomes more advanced and specialised, and at least an intermediate level of chess understanding is assumed. In addition, more attention is paid to how to handle games psychologically. At this stage, increasing use will be made of chess databases and associated software – highly useful for finding the latest successful ideas in a given opening – and computers for analysing one's own games and opening variations. Players are expected to have assimilated an opening repertoire, where the variations they are going to play with White and Black are prepared in advance, studied in great depth and regularly updated.

The presence of a coach will facilitate several aspects of training, including the selection of openings, the identification of weaknesses and means to correct them and the choice of tournaments. A coach will also be valuable in preparing a game against specific opponents, both technically (in particular, the kind of opening variations to choose) and psychologically (for example, for identifying the strengths and weaknesses of the opponent).

The literature about how to progress beyond amateur level used to be dominated by books from the Soviet Union, with some of them still being classics. Admittedly, these books contained a fair amount of Marxist propaganda. For example, after Viktor Korchnoi defected to the West, his games and photographs suddenly disappeared from chess publications released in the USSR. In addition, the selection of games was clearly biased in favour of Soviet players. Nevertheless, these books offered excellent overall quality. Classic examples include Krogius's book on chess psychology, to which I have referred often in the previous chapter, Averbakh's books on endgames and tactics and Kotov's book *Think like a Grandmaster*. This last book provides sophisticated advice about strategy, and rather uniquely, about the proper way of thinking in chess.

Perhaps the most interesting, and to some extent controversial proposal in Kotov's book concerns the way one should calculate variations. Kotov, who was a leading grandmaster in the 1940s and 1950s, notes in the introduction that for many years he was stuck below master level, but then in a matter of two years became a grandmaster. According to him, one of the key reasons for this leap in skill was his realisation that he was calculating variations very inefficiently. He would calculate moves in an unsystematic way, jump from one base move to another, miss important moves and variations, and eventually end up in time trouble where he would make a blunder. A critical analysis of his behaviour led him to conclude that one should first identify candidate moves and then examine them methodically, visiting each branch of the analysis tree only once. Thus, no variation should be double-checked. However, as we have seen in Chapter 3 when discussing progressive deepening, even top grandmasters do visit the same lines several times, and their search is far from being as systematic as computers' search.

So, what's going on? Kotov's method works well in fairly simple positions, but fails when positions are complex, as even the identification of candidate moves is difficult and can indeed be informed by carrying out search. In addition, progressive deepening is a powerful means to overcome limits of short-term memory, as it allows some of the information about the search tree to be encoded in long-term memory, which thereafter can be used as a virtual short-term memory (see Chapter 2). However, for training purposes, Kotov's method is definitively useful. Also, some of the reasons given for not doing progressive deepening (e.g. not trusting one's analysis, tendency to be in time trouble) are likely to be caused by other factors rather than the way search is carried out, such as an inability to make rapid decisions.

Kotov's book also comes with various exercises for improving one's ability to visualise a position and increase depth of search. Most of these exercises boil down to finding the best move in a given position, and are certainly useful. Other authors have proposed to play games blindfold, again to improve one's visualisation skills. In the paper with Peter Jansen mentioned earlier, we were rather critical about this piece of advice. Our argument was that finding good moves and being able to calculate deep variations was primarily the consequence of having acquired considerable knowledge, which allowed players to identify plausible moves rapidly through pattern recognition, not only in the problem situation but also in the positions visualised during look-ahead search. Another point was that, if one has a good understanding of a position, it is often not necessary to anticipate moves very deeply. However, the paper was written for players aiming to become masters, and one could argue that, when one wants to reach higher levels of skill such as grandmaster, playing blindfold games might help fine-tune one's calculating skills.

9

THE MAGIC BULLET?

While most players agree that chess is a fascinating game with endless possibilities and graced with real aesthetic value, there is disagreement about whether it ultimately benefits or penalises those who play it. Siegbert Tarrasch famously wrote that "chess, like love, like music, has the power to make men happy". Some have highlighted possible benefits for education. A quick look at the Internet will display many slogans such as "Chess makes kids smarter" and "Chess improves mathematics". Others have directed attention to the potential costs of playing chess. Orson Wells argued that to destroy a person, you should teach her chess, and George Bernard Shaw asserted that chess "is a foolish expedient for making idle people believe they are doing something very clever when they are only wasting their time". Rare are the activities that have simultaneously inspired such extreme views about their merits and demerits. This chapter deals with the presumed benefits, and the following chapter with the presumed costs.

INSTRUCTIONAL AND COGNITIVE BENEFITS

One common claim is that playing chess improves children's performance in school, in particular with respect to mathematics and language, and generally increases intelligence and other cognitive abilities.

Numerous websites repeat these claims and some authors use them as arguments for advertising the practice of chess. In 2001, the US Chess Trust asked me to review the available evidence, objectively and without any biases. I carried out this review with Guillermo Campitelli. This is obviously a very important topic for the chess world, and a positive answer would have significant implications for education. In fact, it would be a very elegant solution to the difficulties that children and teenagers currently encounter when studying STEM topics.

This question more generally relates to the issue of transfer: can abilities acquired in a particular field (e.g. geometry) generalise to other fields (e.g. science, music) or general abilities (e.g. intelligence, reasoning)? Broadly speaking, there are two types of transfer. With *near transfer*, the two fields overlap, such as geometry and algebra. With *far transfer*, there is no or little overlap between the two fields. An example would be geometry and English. With chess, the strong claim is that there is far transfer.

Establishing the presence of far transfer and thus the causal role of chess raises interesting methodological questions. Three groups are necessary: a treatment group (playing chess, in our case), an active control group (e.g. playing checkers) and a passive control group (no treatment). The active control group is needed in order to control for unspecific factors such as placebo effects and expectations. In addition, participants should be allocated randomly to the three groups. This avoids systematic biases, such as the case where all the more intelligent children are allocated to the chess group whilst the less intelligent children end up in the other two groups. Measures should be taken before the experiment to ensure that the groups do not differ at the outset, and of course after the experiment, to evaluate the effect of treatment. To measure potential changes, the same variables should be measured in the pre-test and the post-test. Such a design in not easy to implement, but is required if one wants to draw strong conclusions about causality: if the treatment group, but not the other two groups, improves on the measure(s) of interest, say ability in mathematics, it is possible to conclude that the effect is specific to some characteristic of the treatment group.

Unfortunately, our review turned out to be rather negative. Although we found many articles extolling the benefits of chess instruction, very few presented empirical evidence, and of those that did, even fewer used a proper experimental design. Only three studies used a design with random assignment and only one study used an active control group. In addition, the few effects that were found (specifically: verbal ability and school performance) differed between the studies and could be due to chance, as a rather large number of measures were taken. Finally, no study collected data about the long-term benefits of chess instruction and information was rarely taken about the characteristics of the teacher. This last omission is important, as in many experiments teachers were highly motivated chess players that were convinced of the cognitive benefits of chess instruction.

A recent review, this time carried out in collaboration with Giovanni Sala, reached the same conclusions. Rather than a narrative review, we carried out a meta-analysis (see Chapter 4) which allowed us to quantify some of the outcomes. A positive result was that the overall quality of the experimental designs had improved over the years, which was reflected by the fact that many studies had been published in peer-reviewed journals, a notable step forward compared to the previous review. However, most of the studies still lacked an active control group, which as we have seen is a necessary safeguard against the presence of non-specific effects.

Based on 24 studies, the results indicated a moderate overall effect size (about one third of a standard deviation). There was a tendency for the effect size to be stronger with mathematics than with reading skills. Also, the effects sizes tended to be stronger with longer instruction. However, caution is required with these results, as no study used an active control group together with random allocation of participants to conditions. In fact, Sala conducted two experiments in his PhD thesis with an active control group (checkers and Go, respectively), and in neither case was there any effect of chess instruction. In addition, a large study conducted by London's Institute of Education in 100 British schools, and involving just over 4,000 children, did not find any effect with respect to performance in mathematics, literacy and science.

Whilst disappointing, these results are not unique to chess. Sala and I carried out similar meta-analyses about the presumed effects of working memory training, music instruction, video-game playing and exergames (video games coupled with physical activity). The results were highly consistent: whilst there was evidence for near transfer, far transfer was very elusive. This pattern of results is well summarised by the title of Sala's PhD thesis: *Once Upon a Time There Was Far Transfer*.

Recently, in part due to the results described in the previous paragraphs, the aims of the chess-in-school movement seem to have shifted. Rather than trying to improve general cognitive abilities and performance in school topics such as mathematics, more modest and realistic goals are targeted, such as using chess to facilitate integration, improve social skills and help children make new friends.

OTHER POTENTIAL BENEFITS

Several authors have argued that chess could be used in psychotherapy. If the patient knows the rules of the game, chess can be used to initiate a therapeutic relation between the psychotherapist and the patient, since it offers the advantage of eschewing verbal interaction, which can be problematic with some individuals. In addition, chess offers a rich symbolism; for example, the promotion of the pawn into a queen when reaching the other side of the board can be seen as a child becoming an adult. In particular with psychoanalytical psychotherapies, this symbolism can be used to express emotions, aggression and other impulses in an acceptable way. More prosaically, it can be used to improve attention and patience, and teach that certain rules must be followed. Unfortunately, there is little empirical evidence on this use of chess. In a short 1949 paper, R. Pakenham-Walsh reports using chess as occupational therapy in a psychiatric hospital. Although the article reports the results of chess matches against local clubs, there is no evaluation of the possible therapeutic benefits of chess.

A project in the Netherlands uses chess with children and adults with an autism spectrum disorder. Chess offers definite advantages here: clear rules, quiet environment and limited physical and social contacts. A recent study reports preliminary results suggesting that playing chess might improve attention deficit hyperactivity disorder (ADHD) symptoms. After an 11-week chess training programme, children with ADHD improved on two measures of their symptoms. A limit of the study is that there was no control group.

It has been proposed that playing chess protects against Alzheimer's and other forms of dementia. The rationale is that playing chess keeps the brain active and builds "cognitive reserve", which increases the chances for the brain to function successfully in spite of structural damage or functional disruption. Unfortunately, preventing dementia has been notably difficult, and a large number of studies have failed to provide unequivocal support for the preventative role of a variety of cognitive activities, including brain training games. A French study followed 3,675 individuals who were dementia-free at the beginning of the study. It was found that individuals playing games such as chess, draughts, card games and bingo were 15% less likely to develop dementia, compared to non-players. However, the effect vanished when baseline measures of cognition and depression were included in the analysis. In addition, the study was correlational, with the usual difficulty in inferring causal links. Thus, since no randomised controlled trial has been carried out with chess, claims about the protective effects of chess playing against dementia must be viewed with great caution.

It has also been proposed that chess could help children from disadvantaged backgrounds, who are at risk of developing drug and crime problems. A large-scale project in New York City and other US cities – the motivation behind the *Knights of the South Bronx* film – found that playing chess increased reading ability. It is indeed impressive to see at-risk children enjoying chess and increasing their chances of completing high school and thus entering universities, against very serious odds. Similarly, in several countries chess is played in prisons. Some inmates enjoy it and are motivated to improve their skills, enhance their self-esteem and make new friends.

These initiatives are inspiring. However, what is lacking for these and similar claims is clear-cut empirical evidence that they are effective. In some cases, there are simply no rigorous scientific evaluations. In addition, the scientific question is to establish whether the benefits are specific to chess, or whether other interventions would work as well. For example, with the chess project contributing to the education of New York City disadvantaged children, it is possible to imagine other interventions that would work, as long as they provide alternatives to crime and drugs, increase kids' self-esteem and offer activities shared by a group. The answer to these questions would not only be theoretically interesting, but would also have practical implications. Before being scientifically confident that the postulated benefits of chess playing are real, it is necessary to collect reliable data. In many cases, this can be done with the kind of methodology that I have discussed with respect to the effects of chess instruction in schools.

Whilst I admire the passion, energy and faith of the persons – mostly but not exclusively chess players – promoting these initiatives, I personally do not think that chess is the magic bullet against the problems facing our society. In my view, chess is a great game providing much excitement, enjoyment and beauty on its own. There is no need to justify its practice by alluding to external benefits.

10

COSTS OF PLAYING CHESS

Observers have not always been sympathetic to chess and some have even noted a number of possible problems with its practice, which can be categorised into two groups: non-psychiatric problems and psychiatric problems. This chapter will address these two categories in turn, with a focus on professional players.

NON-PSYCHIATRIC PROBLEMS

A first obvious cost, which will actually be exacted for any activity in which one wants to excel, is the huge investment of time that is required. By necessity, this will leave little time for other activities. Anecdotal evidence indicates that many chess players aiming to become professionals have left school early, often immediately after obligatory school. And among the players who had a longer education, many started studying at the university but never graduated. This lack of completed education puts professional chess players at a disadvantage if they decide, later in their life, to switch careers.

Although rich in excitement, competitive arousal and fun, a professional chess player's life is also very stressful. There is the obvious tension caused by competitive games, which last for several hours, and tournaments, which last for several days. In addition, few players do really well financially. Perhaps the best 20 players in the world enjoy a high income, and the best 100 players earn a regular income that provides them with long-term financial security. Weaker professionals feel the pinch and their often meagre income depends on winning relatively small amounts of prize money in minor tournaments, teaching, coaching, playing team games and writing books or columns in newspapers. However, competition is fierce and some of these activities will interfere with the kind of practice that is necessary to maintain the level of a strong player.

Chess players often live in rather basic conditions, do a fair amount of travelling – certainly not in business class – and in general adopt a mode of life that is not particularly healthy: poor diet, much alcohol and, for some, smoking. In addition, few players enjoy the security of health insurance or a pension, which means a lack of control about their lives.

This stressful style of life is likely to take its toll. Five former world champions (Morphy, Capablanca, Alekhine, Tal and Petrosian) died fairly young, at the age of 55 years or younger. A 1969 study by Herbert Barry compared strong competitors, weak masters and problem composers, whose activity entails little competition, with respect to their longevity. The strong competitors died at 60 years on average, which was about a decade younger than the individuals in the other two groups. Being world champion was not a reliable predictor, but players who had professional interests unrelated to chess lived longer on average. Given the age of the study, it is a valid question as to whether the conclusions are still correct, although this seems a reasonable assumption.

Blindfold chess, especially simultaneous blindfold chess, has sometimes been singled out as a specific occupational health hazard. For example, Janos Flesh reported that he needed several weeks of rest to recover from blindfold exhibitions with dozens of games. Indeed, such exhibitions were banned in the USSR due to health concerns. Whilst there is no doubt that simultaneous blindfold chess is a strenuous and tiring mental activity, whether it is dangerous is debatable, in particular when sufficient attention has been devoted to preparation.

PSYCHIATRIC PROBLEMS

A common assumption in newspapers, movies and the chess literature is that there is a close link between chess and madness. For example, the 2011 documentary *Bobby Fischer against the World* played with the themes of chess, madness and genius. In *Chess: A Novel*, Stefan Zweig notes that is hard to imagine "a man of intelligence who, without going mad, again and again, over ten, twenty, thirty, forty years, applies the whole elastic power of his thinking to the ridiculous goal of backing a wooden king into the corner of a wooden board!"

The issue of madness is also widespread in the chess psychology literature, and was certainly a central theme in two books written by psychoanalyst Reuben Fine, *The Psychology of the Chess Player* and *Bobby Fischer's Conquest of the World's Chess Championship*. Understanding the presumed link between madness and genius is not unique to chess, and has also been attempted with respect to creativity in music, literature and the visual arts, in what is known as the "mad genius" hypothesis.

There has been much hype in this literature, but some of the cases often discussed are rather straightforward, albeit tragic. For example, there is much mention of an episode where Steinitz was briefly admitted in a psychiatric hospital, amongst other things because he thought he had invented a wireless phone. He was released rapidly and able to conduct a reasonably normal life after, playing in chess tournaments. A few weeks before his death, he was again hospitalised. One account reports that he wanted to play against God through electric communication and give Him the advantage of a pawn and first move. Fine hypothesises that Steinitz was suffering from organic senile psychosis, with some delusional themes relating to his defeat in his world championship match against Lasker.

Similarly, Alekhine was known to drink heavily, which led him to extremes such as being drunk in some of the games of the world championship against Euwe and urinating in public during a simultaneous display. He could also be extremely violent, once destroying the furniture of his hotel room after losing a game. Whether this denotes mental illness is debatable, however. This being said, it is likely the case that some top players suffered from psychiatric diseases. The most often discussed in the literature are Paul Morphy and Bobby Fischer.

Paul Morphy

Paul Charles Morphy was born in 1837. After having learnt to play chess by watching games between his father and uncle, he was one of the best players in New Orleans when he was just 9 years old. At 12, he beat Hungarian master Johann Löwenthal 3–0. However, he did not play much in the following years, devoting himself to his college and later law studies, which he completed brilliantly. When he returned to chess at the age of 20, he won all his games in the first US championship. Since he was not allowed to practice law given his young age, he travelled to Europe and challenged the best players of the world, defeating most of them comprehensively, including Adolf Andersen, the *de facto* world champion.

After his return to Louisiana in 1859 at the age of 22, he totally stopped playing chess. He intended to focus on his career as a lawyer, but the American Civil War (1861–1865) thwarted this plan. He did not manage to restart his law practice after the end of the war, partly because his customers were more interested in discussing chess with him than their legal matters. In spite of this, he lived a comfortable life thanks to the considerable fortune he had inherited from his family. He died at the age of 47 from a stroke, after having taken a cold bath immediately after a long walk on a hot day.

His life was highly organised: daily walk at noon along New Orleans' Canal Street, afternoon with his mother and performance at the opera in the evening. In addition to the fact that he never practiced as a lawyer after the war, some aspects of his life might denote symptoms of psychosis. He incorrectly believed that his brother-in-law had stolen his fortune and wanted to poison him. He methodically organised his shoes in a half-circle. Occasionally, he would stop during his daily walk and rather rudely stare at beautiful women. He also apparently had the habit of walking on his veranda declaiming, in

French, "He will plant the flag of Castille on the walls of Madrid with the cry of the city won and the little king will go away all abashed". However, when his family considered placing him in a sanatorium, Morphy so eloquently defended his legal rights and his sanity that he was sent home.

According to Fine, these idiosyncrasies support the hypothesis that Morphy suffered from paranoia. Following Ernest Jones's earlier analyses (see Chapter 5), he argues that Morphy's symptoms were caused by his rivalry with his father, which was sublimated by playing chess. He notes that Morphy's international successes started one year after the early and unexpected death of his father. In addition, Fine takes Morphy's refusal to consider chess as a profession as an impossibility to accept reality and his extreme confidence in his chess abilities as a sign of exhibitionism. He also proposes that, in his adolescent years, chess succeeded in protected him from psychosis. When he stopped playing chess, this defence disappeared, triggering a psychotic regression.

The soundness of this analysis is debatable. Several biographical details used by Jones and Fine are actually incorrect, as is clear from reading David Lawson's very detailed biography of Morphy. Alternative explanations are not considered, including: the effect of the Civil War on Morphy's mental health, the presence of hereditary causes to his paranoia and the possibility that his decision to stop playing chess might have been caused by the very bad press that chess had in the US at the time, being considered as a type of gambling.

Bobby Fischer

Born in 1943, Fischer was predominantly raised by his mother and rarely saw his father. His childhood was poor and lonely, as his leftist mother was politically engaged and paid relatively little interest to her son. Fischer learnt to play chess at the age of 6, together with his older sister Joan. He progressed very rapidly. At 14, he became US champion and at 15 he become the youngest grandmaster in the world, and indeed the youngest player ever to quality for a candidates' tournament, the penultimate step to win the world title. When he did not qualify as challenger to the world champion, he (correctly) accused Russian players of colluding against Western players (see Chapter 8). Given his chess successes, it is not surprising that he dropped out of high school at the age of 16, arguing that attending school was a waste of time.

Fischer's career was always marred by controversy. For example, he withdrew from the 1967 Sousse interzonal tournament due to the poor way the organisation committee dealt with his observance of the Sabbath, as required by the Seventh-day Adventist Church. When he left the tournament, he was leading with 8½ points out of 10 games. One year later, he refused to play for the US team in the Lugano Olympiad, objecting to the unsatisfactory playing conditions. The real reason might have been that he resented the fact that his fellow American grandmaster Samuel Reshevsky was playing first board for the US.

From 1970 to 1972, he performed at an incredibly high level. First, he won the Palma de Mallorca interzonal tournament with a score of 18½ points out of 23 points, 3½ points ahead of the players finishing joint second. Then, there was 1971, Fischer's miraculous year. In quick succession, he destroyed three of the top players in the world: Taimanov (6–0), Larsen (6–0) and Petrosian (6½ – 2½). The chess world had never seen anything like this. This extraordinary string of victories gave Fischer the right to challenge world champion Boris Spassky.

The match was preceded by complex negotiations, including about its location, which ultimately was agreed to be Reykjavik. Even the day before the official starting date of the match, nobody knew whether Fischer would play. Finally, apparently after being convinced by his friend Anthony Saidy, a chess international master and a medical doctor, he agreed to compete. After losing the first game due to a strange oversight in a basic endgame, he lost the second game by forfeit – as a protest against the noise made by the cameras in the playing room. After this shaky beginning, Fischer started to outclass Spassky with his brilliant play, plethora of new ideas in the openings and continuous psychological pressure. Fischer eventually won the match by 12½ to 8½. After his victory, he withdrew from chess and lived a reclusive life. In particular, he declined to defend his title in 1975, as no agreement about the match conditions could be reached.

It was only in 1992 that he played again, in a controversial match against Spassky that was held in Sveti Stefan and Belgrade. Yugoslavia was at the time under a United Nations embargo, which the US endorsed, and Fischer was thus breaking American law by playing there. It is likely that he did it due to financial pressure: the purse of the match was $5 million, with $3.35 million going to winner. He won the match 17½–12½. It is generally accepted that Fischer, while still playing at a high level, was clearly weaker than the then world champion Garry Kasparov.

Fischer's violation of American law meant that he could not return to the US. He lived in exile in various countries, including Hungary, the Philippines and Japan, until his death in 2008 in Reykjavik, the city where he became world champion. He died from renal failure, after refusing medical treatment from fear of being poisoned, at the symbolic age of 64 (the number of squares on a chessboard).

In his book about the Fischer-Spassky match, Reuben Fine discussed Fischer's psychology at great length. For him, Fischer was "a troubled human being", suffering from "obvious personal problems". Fine and others argued that Fischer displayed several symptoms indicative of paranoia. As evidence for this diagnosis, the following traits are mentioned: his hatred of Jews; his denial of the Holocaust; his accusations that Soviet grandmasters cheated against him; his constant complaints about playing conditions, including lighting, noise and TV cameras; and with one exception, his absence of romantic interaction with women. The last two points merit some comment. Whilst Fischer did complain about playing conditions, he was often justified and was in fact credited with vastly improving the prize money offered to professional chess players. With respect to Fischer's relationships with women, it should be noted that he did have several of them after winning the world championship, including getting married to Miyoko Watai, a Japanese international master.

Fine makes two interesting points about Fischer's mental problems. The first is that, despite his troubled personality and childish behaviour, he was sometimes able to react with maturity and a strong sense of reality to difficult situations. This was the case after the losses incurred in the first two games in his match against Spassky, after which he played superb chess. The second is that, to some extent, chess might have served as the best therapy for Fischer. When he stopped playing after the world championship, his paranoid symptoms increased.

Is there anything to explain?

These hypotheses about the link between chess and madness are intriguing, but also controversial. A first problem is that the quality of the data is poor – anecdotes, personal observations by colleagues, press reports, etc. It is noticeable that Fine, although he personally knew several of the champions he discussed in his books, never carried out a formal and detailed clinical evaluation of any of them.

Second, there is no consideration of base rates. Noting the presence of paranoid personalities, for example, is one thing, but before speculating on any link between genius and madness in chess, one needs to establish that the prevalence of paranoid personalities (or other psychiatric illnesses) in chess is higher than in the general population. Given that the data span two centuries, this is obviously difficult to do, as the prevalence is likely to have changed during this period of time. Similarly, geographical and cultural differences should be taken into account.

Third, and related to the previous point, it is obvious that some of the world champions have lived in extremely difficult conditions – think of the financial duress faced by Steinitz most of his life, and Morphy's experience of the Civil War. Psychoanalytical analyses do not take this into account.

Finally, many of the analyses presented in this chapter are based on psychoanalysis, which has been discredited scientifically and only plays a minor role today in psychology and psychiatry. Specifically, psychoanalytical theories tend to be vague and ill-defined, and it is thus hard if not impossible to test them. Currently, life experiences in childhood and adulthood as well as genetics are considered as more likely causes of mental problems than the kind of explanations adduced by Jones and Fine. In the case of Fischer, a genetic explanation seems very plausible, given that both his parents showed paranoid symptoms.

In general, when considering the current leading grandmasters – say, the top 100 players – there is little, if any, sign of psychiatric illness. To be sure, different personality types are represented, but obviously this does not imply pathological personalities.

11

ENDGAME

We have played a long game and have now reached its final stage. It is time to draw together the different strands of this book.

Researchers now have a fairly good understanding of the topics covered in the first four chapters. We know that perception is central to expertise in chess, knowledge is mostly stored in long-term memory as perceptual chunks linked to possible actions and search is highly selective. We also know that skill in chess mostly finds it origin in a combination of innate factors and dedicated practice. The topics in the second half of the book have been less researched, and less is known about them. They also tend to be more applied and harder to study experimentally.

One theme that has been present in nearly all chapters is that of bounded rationality. Developed in the 1950s by Herbert Simon – whom we have met in several chapters of this book – bounded rationality proposes that humans make decisions that are good enough, but not optimal, because of the limits imposed by their cognitive resources. On the one hand, chess grandmasters choose remarkably good moves: they are nearly always within the first three best moves selected by the top computer engines, and often match the best one. On the other hand, this book has presented substantial empirical evidence that their rationality is limited: their search is extremely selective, covering only a minute portion of the possible search space; they sometimes commit small errors and more rarely are victims of terrible blunders; they cannot transfer their knowledge from chess to other domains; and they can succumb to psychological ruses taking advantage of shortcomings of their style. More controversially, other aspects of chess psychology can be taken as evidence for bounded rationality: the need to cheat for winning games and the suboptimal contact with reality displayed by some players.

In the end, chess has been true to its reputation of drosophila of cognition. It has much contributed to our understanding of human cognition, not the least because it is both a closed and complex world. This will continue to be the case in the future, with new methods and new scientific questions.

FURTHER READING

Barry, H. (1969). Longevity of outstanding chess players. *Journal of Genetic Psychology*, 115, 143–148.

This article provides data showing that leading chess players have a shorter life expectancy than weaker players.

Bilalić, M., McLeod, P., & Gobet, F. (2010). The mechanism of the Einstellung (set) effect: A pervasive source of cognitive bias. *Current Directions in Psychological Science*, 19, 111–115.

This article provides an overview of the experiments carried out on set effects in chess. Particularly revealing is the experiment using eye-movement recording.

Bilalić, M., Smallbone, K., Mcleod, P., & Gobet, F. (2009). Why are (the best) women so good at chess? Participation rates and gender differences in intellectual domains. *Proceedings of the Royal Society B*, 276, 1161–1165.

Based on a statistical analysis, this article argues that participation rates should be taken into account before other explanations for the presence of gender differences in chess are considered.

Blasco-Fontecilla, H., et al. (2016). Efficacy of chess training for the treatment of ADHD: A prospective, open label study. *Revista de Psiquiatría y Salud Mental*, 9, 13–21.

This study uses chess for reducing symptoms of ADHD.

Burgoyne, A. P., Sala, G., Gobet, F., Macnamara, B. N., Campitelli, G., & Hambrick, D. Z. (2016). The relationship between cognitive ability and chess skill: A comprehensive meta-analysis. *Intelligence*, 59, 72–83.

> This meta-analysis clearly shows that expertise in chess is related to intelligence.

Campitelli, G., & Gobet, F. (2004). Adaptive expert decision making: Skilled chess players search more and deeper. *Journal of the International Computer Games Association*, 27, 209–216.

> In the experiment reported in this paper, participants had to solve fiendishly complicated problems. The verbal protocols revealed very clear-cut skill differences in the amount of search that was carried out.

Campitelli, G., Gobet, F., & Bilalić, M. (2014). Cognitive processes and development of chess genius: An integrative approach. In D. K. Simonton (Ed.), *The Wiley handbook of genius* (pp. 350–374). Chichester, UK: Wiley-Blackwell.

> This book chapter describes a model of the interaction of practice and talent in chess and derives predictions through mathematical simulations.

Charness, N. (1976). Memory for chess positions: Resistance to interference. *Journal of Experimental Psychology: Human Learning and Memory*, 2, 641–653.

> This article presents several experiments showing that memory for briefly presented chess positions is unaffected by interpolated tasks. This result challenges chunking theory.

Charness, N., Reingold, E. M., Pomplun, M., & Stampe, D. M. (2001). The perceptual aspect of skilled performance in chess: Evidence from eye movements. *Memory & Cognition*, 29, 1146–1152.

> This article provides interesting data on the role of eye movements when chess players try to find the best move in a position.

Chassy, P. & Gobet, F. (2010). Speed of expertise acquisition depends upon inherited factors. *Talent Development and Excellence*, 2, 17–27.

> This article proposes a genetic hypothesis that accounts for inter-individual differences in the acquisition of expertise.

Dartigues, J. F., et al. (2013). Playing board games, cognitive decline and dementia: A French population-based cohort study. *BMJ Open*, 3.

> This is a large study looking at the possible benefits of playing board games and other games for reducing the risk of dementia.

De Groot, A. D. (1978). *Thought and choice in chess* (2nd English ed.; 1st Dutch ed. in 1946). The Hague: Mouton Publishers.

De Groot's *magnum opus* is a must for anybody interested in chess psychology. The book focuses on chess players' thinking processes when they choose a move, but also discusses the role of perception and memory.

De Groot, A. D., Gobet, F., & Jongman, R. W. (1996). *Perception and memory in chess: Heuristics of the professional eye.* Assen: Van Gorcum.

This systematic study of the role of perception in chess provides detailed analyses of eye-movement data. It also discusses findings and theories on memory. In the last chapter, the first two authors defend their different views about the nature of intuition in chess.

Dreyfus, H. L., & Dreyfus, S. E. (1986). *Mind over machine.* New York, NY: Free Press.

This book presents the influential five-stage theory of intuition. Chess is used repeatedly to support the authors' argument.

Ericsson, K. A., Krampe, R. T., & Tesch-Römer, C. (1993). The role of deliberate practice in the acquisition of expert performance. *Psychological Review, 100,* 363–406.

This is the key paper on deliberate practice. It focuses on music, but also uses chess as a source of evidence.

Euwe, M. (1978). *The development of chess style.* New York, NY: David McKay.

This book presents the thesis that the development of players' individual style parallels the historical development of styles.

Ferrari, V., Didierjean, A., & Marmèche, E. (2006). Dynamic perception in chess. *Quarterly Journal of Experimental Psychology, 59,* 397–410.

This article presents two fascinating experiments showing that anticipatory schemas might lead to errors.

Fine, R. (1967). *The psychology of the chess player.* New York, NY: Dover.

This is the classic but controversial application of Freudian psychoanalysis for explaining chess players' unconscious motivations.

Fine, R. (1973). *Bobby Fischer's conquest of the world's chess championship: The psychology and tactics of the title match.* New York, NY: David McKay.

This book discusses the application of psychoanalytical theory to the match of the century.

Gobet, F. (2016). *Understanding expertise: A multidisciplinary approach.* London: Palgrave.

This is a comprehensive discussion of research into expertise. Since chess has much contributed to the topic, it is covered in some detail, not only from the point of view of psychology, but also from the point of views of neuroscience, philosophy and artificial intelligence.

Gobet, F., & Campitelli, G. (2006). Education and chess: A critical review. In T. Redman (Ed.), *Chess and education: Selected essays from the Koltanowski conference* (pp. 124–143). Dallas, TX: Chess Program at the University of Texas at Dallas.
This book chapter reviews the research using chess for improving cognitive abilities and educational achievement. It provides a detailed discussion on the ideal methodology to use for carrying out this type of research.

Gobet, F., & Campitelli, G. (2007). The role of domain-specific practice, handedness and starting age in chess. *Developmental Psychology, 43*, 159–172.
This is one of the first papers to challenge the deliberate practice framework with the kind of empirical data used by this approach. Its contribution was also to combine data on deliberate practice with data on talent.

Gobet, F., & Chassy, P. (2009). Expertise and intuition: A tale of three theories. *Minds & Machines, 19*, 151–180.
This article presents a critique of Simon and Chase's and Dreyfus and Dreyfus's theories of intuition, and proposes a new theory, based on template theory (see Chapter 2).

Gobet, F., de Voogt, A. J., & Retschitzki, J. (2004). *Moves in mind*. Hove, UK: Psychology Press.
This book presents a systematic review of the psychology of board games, with particular attention to chess.

Gobet, F., & Jansen, P. J. (2006). Training in chess: A scientific approach. In T. Redman (Ed.), *Chess and education: Selected essays from the Koltanowski conference* (pp. 81–97). Dallas, TX: Chess Program at the University of Texas at Dallas.
This book chapter uses results in cognitive psychology to develop principles of chess instruction.

Gobet, F., Lane, P. C. R., Croker, S., Cheng, P. C. H., Jones, G., Oliver, I., & Pine, J. M. (2001). Chunking mechanisms in human learning. *Trends in Cognitive Sciences, 5*, 236–243.
This is a review showing the general role of chunking mechanisms in human cognition, beyond chess. It provides a brief presentation of the CHREST model.

Gobet, F., & Simon, H. A. (1996). The roles of recognition processes and look-ahead search in time-constrained expert problem solving: Evidence from grandmaster level chess. *Psychological Science, 7*, 52–55.
This paper analyses world champion Garry Kasparov's simultaneous exhibitions against national teams and the team of Hamburg. It takes

Kasparov's remarkable results as support for the role of pattern recognition in chess skill and expertise in general.

Gobet, F., & Simon, H. A. (1996). Templates in chess memory: A mechanism for recalling several boards. *Cognitive Psychology*, 31, 1–40.

This article describes experiments challenging chunking theory and presents a revision of this theory.

Guid, M., & Bratko, I. (2006). Computer analysis of chess champions. *ICGA Journal*, 29, 65–73.

This fascinating but also contentious article uses computer analyses to study the style of world champions.

Halpern, D. F. (2013). *Sex differences in cognitive abilities* (4th ed.). New York, NY: Psychology Press.

Diane Halpern is the world expert on gender differences in cognition. The book systematically reviews the empirical evidence and the theories that have been proposed to explain it. Recommended if you are interested in gender differences.

Hearst, E., & Knott, J. (2009). *Blindfold chess: History, psychology, techniques, champions, world records and important games.* Jefferson, NC: McFarland.

This book presents a systematic review of the literature on blindfold chess.

Holding, D. H. (1985). *The psychology of chess skill.* Hillsdale, NJ: Erlbaum.

In this book, Holding criticises Simon and Chase's chunking theory and their emphasis on pattern recognition, and argues rather that the ability to look-ahead is the main factor in chess skill.

Kotov, A. (1971). *Think like a grandmaster.* London: Batsford.

This classic in the chess literature provides advice for ambitious players about how to become a grandmaster. The emphasis is on developing discipline for calculating variations.

Krogius, N. (1976). *Psychology in chess.* London: R. H. M Press.

This book is another classic in the chess literature. Nicolai Krogius describes a large number of competitive games where psychology played an important role. The book rarely refers to the scientific literature, but the author demonstrates a very good understanding of human psychology.

Lawson, D. (1976). *The pride and sorrow of chess.* New York, NY: David McKay.

This is the definitive biography of Paul Morphy.

Maass, A., D'Ettole, C., & Cadinu, M. (2008). Checkmate? The role of gender stereotypes in the ultimate intellectual sport. *European Journal of Social Psychology*, 38, 231–245.

> The article argues that male domination in chess is due to gender stereotypes.

Moul, C. C., & Nye, J. V. (2006). Did the Soviets collude? A statistical analysis of championship chess 1940–64. Retrieved from http://dx.doi.org/10.2139/ssrn.905612.

> An interesting statistical analysis that supports Bobby Fischer's claim that Soviet grandmasters essentially cheated against Western players.

Murray, H. J. R. (1952). *A history of chess* (reprint of the 1913 ed.). New York, NY: Skyhorse Publishing Press.

> First published in 1913, this is the definitive reference on the history of chess.

Polgár, L. (2017). *Raise a genius!* (Original ed. in Hungarian, 1989). Translation and copyright: Gordon Tisher.

> In this book, László Pogar presents his views on education and describes the "experiment" he and his wife carried out on their three daughters. For many years, the book was available only in Hungarian and Esperanto. It can be downloaded at http://slatestarcodex.com/Stuff/genius.pdf.

Saariluoma, P. (1992). Error in chess: The apperception-restructuring view. *Psychological Research*, 54, 17–26.

> This paper describes elegant studies where errors are induced experimentally.

Saariluoma, P. (1995). *Chess players' thinking: A cognitive psychological approach.* London: Routledge.

> This book discusses the psychology of chess, with a focus on the author's research. Experiments on blindfold chess are discussed in some detail.

Sala, G., & Gobet, F. (2016). Do the benefits of chess instruction transfer to academic and cognitive skills? A meta-analysis. *Educational Research Review*, 46–57.

> This meta-analysis statistically combines the results of 24 studies.

Silver, D., et al. (2016). Mastering the game of Go with deep neural networks and tree search. *Nature*, 529, 484–489.

> AlphaGo, which is described in this paper, revolutionised the way computers play Go.

Simon, H. A., & Chase, W. G. (1973). Skill in chess. *American Scientist*, 61, 393–403.
In this classic paper, Simon and Chase provide an overview of the seminal research they carried out on chess.

Stafford, T. (2018). Female chess players outperform expectations when playing men. *Psychological Science*, 29, 429–436.
Using data from a large database, this article argues that women do not suffer from any stereotype threat, but rather play better than expected when facing men.

Printed in the United States
by Baker & Taylor Publisher Services